Books by Laurie Blum

<u>Childcare/Education</u>

FREE MONEY FOR GRADUATE SCHOOL
FREE MONEY FROM COLLEGES AND UNIVERSITIES
FREE MONEY FOR ATHLETIC SCHOLARSHIPS
FREE MONEY FOR COLLEGE FROM THE GOVERNMENT
FREE MONEY FOR DAY CARE
FREE MONEY FOR PRIVATE SCHOOLS
FREE MONEY FOR FOREIGN STUDY
FREE MONEY FOR COLLEGE
FREE MONEY FOR CHILDREN'S MEDICAL EXPENSES
FREE MONEY FOR CHILDHOOD BEHAVIORAL AND GENETIC DISORDERS

<u>Healthcare</u>

FREE MONEY FOR HEART DISEASE AND CANCER CARE
FREE MONEY FOR DISEASES OF AGING
FREE MONEY FOR INFERTILITY TREATMENTS
FREE MONEY FOR MENTAL/EMOTIONAL DISORDERS

<u>The Arts</u>

FREE MONEY FOR PEOPLE IN THE ARTS

<u>Business</u>

FREE MONEY FOR SMALL BUSINESS AND ENTREPRENEURS
HOW TO INVEST IN REAL ESTATE USING FREE MONEY
FREE MONEY FROM THE FEDERAL GOVERNMENT
FOR SMALL BUSINESSES AND ENTREPRENEURS

<u>Other</u>

FREE DOLLARS FROM THE FEDERAL GOVERNMENT
THE COMPLETE GUIDE TO GETTING A GRANT

Free Money for Athletic Scholarships

Laurie Blum

A Henry Holt Reference Book

Henry Holt and Company

New York

A Henry Holt Reference Book
Henry Holt and Company, Inc.
Publishers since 1866
115 West 18th Street
New York, New York 10011

Henry Holt ® is a registered trademark
of Henry Holt and Company, Inc.

Published in Canada by Fitzhenry & Whiteside Ltd.,
195 Allstate Parkway, Markham, Ontario L3R 4T8.

Library of Congress Cataloging-in-Publication Data
Blum, Laurie.
          Free money for athletic scholarships / Laurie Blum. — 1st ed.
          p. cm. — (A Henry Holt reference book) (Free money series)
     Includes index.
     1. Sports—Scholarships, fellowships, etc.—United States—Directories.
     I. Title. II. Series: Blum, Laurie. Free money series.
     GV583.B56   1993   93-4265
     796'.079—dc20   CIP
ISBN 0-8050-2659-2
ISBN 0-8050-2660-6 (An Owl Book: pbk.)

Henry Holt books are available for special promotions and premiums.
For details contact: Director, Special Markets.

First Edition—1993

Designed by Christina M. Riley
Printed in the United States of America
All first editions are printed on acid-free paper. ∞

1 3 5 7 9 10 8 6 4 2
1 3 5 7 9 10 8 6 4 2
(pbk.)

I would like to briefly but sincerely thank Beth Martin Brown, Cybèle Fisher, Walter Goldenberg, Ken Rose, Sylvia Szeker, my wonderful editor Paula Kakalecik, Christina M. Riley, Ron Stone and Ken Wright.

Contents

. . . .

Introduction

• • • • • • • • • • • • • • • • • • • •

Many millions of dollars in athletic scholarships go unclaimed each year simply because no one applied for them, or because the athletic departments couldn't find enough qualified applicants.

Before you put down this book because you are not a 250 pound left tackle, or do not have the backhand of Steffi Graf, consider the following:

Until the late 1970's it was all too common for colleges to have multimillion dollar training facilities for the football and basketball teams, while the women's volleyball team practiced on a muddy lot with a clothesline stretched between two poles. A law that took effect in 1978 decreed that schools must provide male and female athletes with "equal benefits and opportunities." That means separate but equal practice facilities, equipment, number of coaches, number of games and scholarship money.

In the late 1970's and early 1980's, the sports pages were filled with tales of academic abuses committed by outstanding athletes. There are now restrictions on how poorly the star quarterback can do academically before he is asked to leave school. One of the results of these scandals is the limit imposed by a school on how many scholarships can be awarded in the "major" sports (football, basketball, track and field, softball) with requirements that money be distributed among women athletes in these sports, as well as in archery, badminton, bowling, crew, Frisbee (yes, there is a scholarship currently available at the State University of New York at Purchase, albeit just one), handball, and synchronized swimming.

Schools are not restricted in how they spend their recruiting time and effort, only their scholarship money. Consequently, they will often devote a considerable amount of time and effort seeking out the best basketball and football players, but pay little or no attention to seeking out the best archery, bowling or lacrosse athletes. If someone happens to turn up and ask for scholarship money, fine. If not, the money goes back into the general fund. So be sure not to neglect some of your less obvious skills; one of them might help pay for your college education.

The book is divided into two parts. The first section lists colleges and universities in all fifty states that give athletic scholarships to students. Wherever possible I have listed the various sports for which scholarships are given, the number of scholarships given, the average size of an award, the range of monies given, and who to contact. The listings are arranged alphabetically by school within each state. The second section lists sports associations, some of which award scholarships as well as others that though they do not give outright awards, I thought would be useful for the college athlete as they sponsor tournaments, competitions, coaching clinics and seminars. Check both sections to see what listings apply to you.

How to Apply

There are NCAA rules and regulations for different size schools which dictate how many awards can be given out and in which sports. Colleges and universities belong to different divisions which have their own rules and guidelines for athletic scholarships. Division I and I AA have what are called "head count sports" which receive full scholarships. Division II schools give "partial awards" which usually consist of partial tuition payment or grants to cover books or part of an athlete's room and board. Division III schools do not give any athletic awards. Usually individual coaches of various sports recruit the students they'd like to see play at their respective schools. Students who want to apply to the schools directly must contact the individual coach of the particular sport they're interested in. If the student is accepted at the school, in many cases financial aid packages are worked out by both a financial aid officer and the head coach. Many times, the athletic coaches only have a certain amount of money in their budgets to divide among many athletes with financial need. Therefore, dispersement of funds is discretionary; that is, there are not a set number of awards. Rather, hopefully, there will be partial scholarships divided amongst all the athletes with financial need.

One Final Note

By the time this book is published, some of the information
contained here will have changed. No reference book can be
as up to date as the reader or author would like. Names,
addresses, dollar amounts, telephone numbers, and other
data are always in flux; however, most of the information will
not have changed. Good luck!

Free Money for Athletic Scholarships

College and University Scholarships

ALABAMA

Alabama Agriculture and Mechanical University
Normal, AL 35762
(205) 851-5360

Description: Athletic scholarships for undergraduates
Restrictions: Limited to scholarships for men's and women's basketball, men's cross country, football and soccer, men's and women's swimming, men's tennis, women's track and field and volleyball
$ Given: 61 grants for men, 19 grants for women; average range: $350-$1550 (full tuition)
Deadline: Contact the department coach
Contact: Mr. Gene Bright, Athletic Director

Auburn University
Auburn, AL 36849
(205) 844-4750

Description: Athletic scholarships for undergraduates
Restrictions: Limited to scholarships for men's baseball, men's and women's basketball, cross country and diving, men's football, men's and women's golf, women's gymnastics, men's and women's swimming, tennis and track and field and women's volleyball
$ Given: Unspecified number of awards ranging: $200-$8,591 (full tuition)
Deadline: Contact the department coach
Contact: Mr. Milo R. Lewd, Athletic Director

FREE MONEY FOR ATHLETIC SCHOLARSHIPS

• • • • • • • • • • • • • • • • • • • •

Auburn University at Montgomery
Atlantic Highway
Montgomery, AL 36193
(205) 271-9300

Description: Athletic scholarships for undergraduates
Restrictions: Limited to scholarships for men's baseball, men's and women's basketball, men's soccer, men's and women's tennis
$ Given: Unspecified number of awards
Deadline: Contact the department coach
Contact: Mr. Larry Chapman, Athletic Director

Birmingham-Southern College
800 8th Avenue
Birmingham, AL 35254
(205) 226-4640

Description: Athletic scholarships for undergraduates
Restrictions: Limited to scholarships for men's basketball and soccer, men's and women's tennis
$ Given: Unspecified number of awards
Deadline: Contact the department coach
Contact: Dr. Rob Moxley, Athletic Director and Vice President of Business Affairs

Huntingdon College
1500 East Fairview Avenue
Montgomery, AL 36106
(205) 265-0511

Description: Athletic scholarships for undergraduates
Restrictions: Limited to scholarships for men's baseball and golf, men's and women's soccer, women's softball, men's and women's tennis, women's volleyball
$ Given: Unspecified number of awards
Deadline: Contact the department coach
Contact: Mr. Todd Schilperoort, Director of the Athletic Department

Livingston University
Washington Street
Livingston, AL 35470
(205) 652-9661

Description: Athletic scholarships for undergraduates
Restrictions: Limited to scholarships for men's baseball, men's and women's basketball, men's football and golf, women's softball, men's and women's tennis, women's volleyball
$ Given: 94 grants for men totaling $106,000, 38 grants for women totaling $44,000; average range: $200-$4,300 (full tuition)
Deadline: Contact the department coach
Contact: Dr. Billy Slay, Athletic Director

. . . .

Mobile College
Mobile, AL 36613
(205) 675-5990

Description: Athletic scholarships for undergraduates
Restrictions: Limited to scholarships for men's baseball, men's and women's basketball and cross country, men's golf and soccer, women's softball, men's and women's tennis
$ Given: Unspecified number of awards ranging: $200-$6,800 (full tuition)
Deadline: Contact the department coach
Contact: Dr. Bill Elder, Athletic Director

Samford University
800 Lakeshore Drive
Birmingham, AL 35209
(205) 870-2966

Description: Athletic scholarships for undergraduates
Restrictions: Limited to scholarships for men's baseball, basketball, cross country, football and golf, women's gymnastics and softball, men's and women's track and field and volleyball
$ Given: 21 grants for men, 18 grants for women; average range: Up to $10,942 (full tuition)
Deadline: Contact the department coach
Contact: Mr. Steven Allgood, Director of the Athletic Department

Springhill College
Mobile, AL 36608
(205) 460-2346

Description: Athletic scholarships for undergraduates
Restrictions: Limited to scholarships for men's baseball, men's and women's basketball, women's cross country, men's and women's golf, men's and women's tennis
$ Given: 14 grants for men totaling $58,096, 9 grants for women totaling $37,875; average range: $1,000-$16,800 (full tuition)
Deadline: Contact the department coach
Contact: Mr. Carl Nash, Athletic Director

FREE MONEY FOR ATHLETIC SCHOLARSHIPS

• •

Talladega College
627 West Battle Street
Talladega, AL 35160
(205) 362-0206

Description: Athletic scholarships for undergraduates
Restrictions: Limited to scholarships for men's baseball, men's and women's basketball and track and field
$ Given: Unspecified number of awards ranging: $500-$8,300 (full tuition)
Deadline: Contact the department coach
Contact: Mr. Wylie Tucker, Athletic Director

Troy State University
Troy, AL 36081
(205) 670-3000

Description: Athletic scholarships for undergraduates
Restrictions: Limited to scholarships for men's baseball, men's and women's basketball, men's cross country, football and golf, men's and women's tennis, men's track and field, women's volleyball
$ Given: Unspecified number of awards
Deadline: Contact the department coach
Contact: Dr. Kennith Blankenship, Athletic Director

Tuskegee University
Tuskegee, AL 36088
(205) 727-8849

Description: Athletic scholarships for undergraduates
Restrictions: Limited to scholarships for men's baseball, men's and women's basketball, men's football, men's and women's tennis and track and field, women's volleyball
$ Given: 53 grants for men totaling $82,000, 4 grants for women totaling $18,000; average range: Up to $10,000 (full tuition)
Deadline: Contact the department coach
Contact: Mr. James Martin, Athletic Director

University of Alabama at Birmingham
University Station
Birmingham, AL 35294
(205) 934-3402 (M)
(205) 934-7252 (W)

Description: Athletic scholarships for undergraduates
Restrictions: Limited to scholarships for men's baseball, men's and women's basketball and cross country and golf, men's riflery and soccer, women's track and field and volleyball
$ Given: 14 grants for men, 12 grants for women; average range: $200-$7,500 (full tuition)
Deadline: Contact the department coach
Contact: Mr. Gene Bartow, Athletic Director

University of Alabama in Huntsville
Huntsville, AL 35899
(205) 895-6144

Description: Athletic scholarships for undergraduates
Restrictions: Limited to scholarships for men's and women's basketball, crew and cross country, men's golf, ice hockey and soccer, men's and women's tennis, women's volleyball
$ Given: Unspecified number of awards ranging: $200-$3,600 (full tuition)
Deadline: Contact the department coach
Contact: Mr. Paul Brand, Director of the Athletic Department

University of Alabama at Tuscaloosa
P.O. Box 870162
Tuscaloosa, AL 35487
(205) 348-3600

Description: Athletic scholarships for undergraduates
Restrictions: Limited to scholarships for men's baseball, men's and women's basketball and cross country, men's diving and football, men's and women's golf, women's gymnastics, men's and women's swimming, swimming-diving, tennis and track and field
$ Given: 54 grants for men totaling $285,149, 49 scholarships for women totaling $190,778; average range: $200-$9,000 (full tuition)
Deadline: Contact the department coach
Contact: Dr. Gary White, Associate Athletic Director

University of Montevallo
Montevallo, AL 35115
(205) 665-6600

Description: Athletic scholarships for undergraduates
Restrictions: Limited to scholarships for men's baseball, men's and women's basketball, men's golf, women's volleyball
$ Given: Unspecified number of awards ranging: Up to $7,074 (full tuition)
Deadline: Contact the department coach
Contact: Mr. Rob Spivery, Athletic Director

FREE MONEY FOR ATHLETIC SCHOLARSHIPS

• •

University of South Alabama
307 University Boulevard
Mobile, AL 36688
(205) 460-7121

Description: Athletic scholarships for undergraduates
Restrictions: Limited to scholarships for men's baseball, men's and women's basketball, cross country and golf, men's soccer, men's and women's tennis and track and field, women's volleyball
$ Given: 28 grants for men, 16 grants for women; average range: Up to $4,500 (full tuition)
Deadline: Contact the department coach
Contact: Mr. Joe Gottlieb, Athletic Director

ALASKA

University of Alaska Anchorage
3211 Providence Drive
Anchorage, AK 99508
(907) 786-1230

Description: Athletic scholarships for undergraduates
Restrictions: Limited to scholarships for men's and women's alpine skiing and basketball, men's cross country, men's and women's cross country skiing, women's gymnastics, men's ice hockey, swimming, swimming-diving, women's volleyball
$ Given: 5 grants for men totaling $30,590, 5 grants for women totaling $30,590
Deadline: Contact the department coach
Contact: Mr. Tim Dillon, Athletic Director

University of Alaska Fairbanks
Fairbanks, AK 99775-0240
(907) 474-7205

Description: Athletic scholarships for undergraduates
Restrictions: Limited to scholarships for men's and women's basketball, cross country, country skiing, diving, riflery and swimming, women's volleyball
$ Given: Unspecified number of awards ranging: $500-$4,992
Deadline: Contact the department coach
Contact: Ms. Lynn Lashbrook, Athletic Director

ARIZONA

Arizona State University
Tempe, AZ 85287-0412
(602) 965-3482

Description: Athletic scholarships for undergraduates
Restrictions: Limited to scholarships for men's and women's archery and badminton, men's baseball, men's and women's basketball, cross country and diving, men's football, men's and women's golf and gymnastics, women's softball, men's and women's swimming, swimming-diving, tennis and track and field, women's volleyball, men's wrestling
$ Given: 79 grants for men totaling $193,750, 50 grants for women totaling $106,250; average range: Up to $8,152 (full tuition)
Deadline: Contact the department coach
Contact: Mr. Charles Harris, Athletic Director

Grand Canyon University
3300 West Camelback
Phoenix, AZ 85017
(602) 249-3300

Description: Athletic scholarships for undergraduates
Restrictions: Limited to scholarships for men's and women's basketball, men's golf, men's and women's soccer and tennis, women's volleyball
$ Given: 11 grants for men, 5 grants for women ('92-'93); average range: $200-$10,358 (full tuition)
Deadline: Contact the department coach
Contact: Mr. Gil Stafford, Athletic Director

Northern Arizona University
Box 15400
Flagstaff, AZ 86001
(602) 523-5353

Description: Athletic scholarships for undergraduates
Restrictions: Limited to scholarships for men's and women's basketball and cross country, women's diving, men's football and ice hockey, women's swimming and swimming-diving, men's and women's tennis and track and field, women's volleyball, men's wrestling
$ Given: 140 grants for men totaling $462,800, 83 grants for women totaling $254,207; average range: $210-$9,880 (full tuition)
Deadline: Contact the department coach
Contact: Mr. Tom George, Director of Athletics

FREE MONEY FOR ATHLETIC SCHOLARSHIPS

• •

University of Arizona
Tucson, AZ 85721
(602) 621-2200

Description: Athletic scholarships for undergraduates
Restrictions: Limited to scholarships for men's baseball, men's and women's basketball and cross country, men's football, men's and women's golf, women's gymnastics and softball, men's and women's swimming-diving, tennis and track and field, women's volleyball
$ Given: 31 grants for men totaling $123,725, 10 grants for women totaling $49,520; average range: Up to $7,350 (full tuition)
Deadline: Contact the department coach
Contact: Dr. Cedric Dempfey, Athletic Director

ARKANSAS

Arkansas College
2300 Highland Road
Batesville, AR 72501
(501) 793-9813

Description: Athletic scholarships for undergraduates
Restrictions: Limited to scholarships for men's and women's basketball, cross country, golf and track and field
$ Given: Unspecified number of awards ranging: $4,000-$8,016 (full tuition)
Deadline: Contact the department coach
Contact: Mr. Terry Garner, Athletic Director

Arkansas State University
State University, AR 72467
(501) 972-3880

Description: Athletic scholarships for undergraduates
Restrictions: Limited to scholarships for men's baseball, men's and women's basketball and cross country, men's golf, women's tennis, men's and women's track and field, women's volleyball
$ Given: Unspecified number of awards ranging: $1,500-$3,000
Deadline: Contact the department coach
Contact: Charles Thorton, Athletic Director

• • • • • • • • • • • • • • • • • • • •

Arkansas Technical University
Highway 7
Russellville, AR 72801
(501) 968-0345

Description: Athletic scholarships for undergraduates
Restrictions: Limited to scholarships for men's baseball, men's and women's basketball, men's football and golf, men's and women's tennis
$ Given: 65 grants for men totaling $205,170, 21 grants for women totaling $70,000; average range: Up to $5,435 (full tuition)
Deadline: Contact the department coach
Contact: Mr. Don Sevier, Athletic Director

Harding University
900 East Center
Searcy, AR 72143
(501) 268-616

Description: Athletic scholarships for undergraduates
Restrictions: Limited to scholarships for men's baseball, men's and women's basketball and cross country, men's football and tennis, men's and women's track and field, women's volleyball
$ Given: 9 grants for men, 6 grants for women; average range: $4,000-$8,000 (full tuition)
Deadline: Contact the department coach
Contact: Dr. Harry Olree, Director of the Athletic Department

Henderson State University
Box 7627
Arkadelphia, AR 71923
(501) 246-5511

Description: Athletic scholarships for undergraduates
Restrictions: Limited to scholarships for men's and women's basketball, men's football, women's volleyball
$ Given: 18 grants for men totaling $42,400, 10 grants for women totaling $29,380; average range: $250-$3,100 (full tuition)
Deadline: Contact the department coach
Contact: Mr. Ken Turner, Athletic Director

FREE MONEY FOR ATHLETIC SCHOLARSHIPS

• •

John Brown University
Siloam Springs, AR 72761
(501) 524-3131

Description: Athletic scholarships for undergraduates
Restrictions: Limited to scholarships for men's and women's basketball, men's soccer, men's and women's swimming, swimming-diving and tennis, women's volleyball
$ Given: 18 grants for men totaling $42,400, 10 grants for women totaling $29,380; average range: $500-$9,000 (full tuition)
Deadline: Contact the department coach
Contact: Mr. Jack Augustine, Sports Information Director

Ouachita Baptist University
410 Ouachita Street
Arkadelphia, AR 71923
(501) 245-5181

Description: Athletic scholarships for undergraduates
Restrictions: Limited to scholarships for men's and women's basketball, men's football, women's volleyball
$ Given: 21 grants for men totaling $78,000, 7 grants for women totaling $26,000; average range: $4,200-$8,400 (full tuition)
Deadline: Contact the department coach
Contact: Mr. Bill Vining, Athletic Director

University of Arkansas at Little Rock
Little Rock, AR 72204
(501) 569-3130

Description: Athletic scholarships for undergraduates
Restrictions: Limited to scholarships for men's baseball and basketball, men's and women's cross country, men's diving, men's and women's soccer, swimming and tennis, women's track and field and volleyball
$ Given: Unspecified number of awards ranging: Up to $4,000 (full tuition)
Deadline: Contact the department coach
Contact: Mr. Mike Hammerick, Athletic Director

University of Arkansas at Monticello
Monticello, AR
(501) 460-1058

Description: Athletic scholarships for undergraduates
Restrictions: Limited to scholarships for men's and women's basketball, men's football
$ Given: 9 grants for men, 6 grants for women; average range: $250-$3,600 (full tuition)
Deadline: Contact the department coach
Contact: Lawrence Smithmier, Director of the Athletic Department

University of Arkansas at Pine Bluff
Pine Bluff, AR 71601
(501) 543-8657

Description: Athletic scholarships for undergraduates
Restrictions: Limited to scholarships for men's and women's basketball, men's football, women's volleyball
$ Given: Unspecified number of awards ranging: Up to $3,140 (full tuition)
Deadline: Contact the department coach
Contact: Mr. H.O. Clemmons, Athletic Director

University of Central Arkansas
Conway, AR 72032
(501) 450-3150

Description: Athletic scholarships for undergraduates
Restrictions: Limited to scholarships for men's and women's basketball, men's football, women's volleyball
$ Given: 12 grants for men, 10 grants for women; average range: $525-$2,100 (full tuition)
Deadline: Contact the department coach
Contact: Mr. Bill Stevens, Athletic Director

CALIFORNIA

Azusa Pacific College
Azusa, CA 91702
(818) 969-3434

Description: Athletic scholarships for undergraduates
Restrictions: Limited to scholarships for men's baseball, men's and women's basketball and cross country, men's football, men's and women's soccer, women's softball, men's tennis, men's and women's track and field, women's volleyball
$ Given: Unspecified number of awards
Deadline: Contact the department coach
Contact: Dr. Cliff Hamlow, Athletic Director

FREE MONEY FOR ATHLETIC SCHOLARSHIPS

• •

Biola University
La Mirada, CA 90639
(310) 944-0351

Description: Athletic scholarships for undergraduates
Restrictions: Limited to scholarships for men's baseball, men's and women's basketball and cross country, men's soccer, women's tennis, men's and women's track and field, women's volleyball
$ Given: Unspecified number of awards; average range $1,000-$4,000
Deadline: Contact the department coach
Contact: Dr. David Holmquist, Athletic Director

California Baptist College
Riverside, CA 92504
(714) 689-5771

Description: Athletic scholarships for undergraduates
Restrictions: Limited to scholarships for men's baseball, men's and women's basketball, men's soccer, women's softball, men's tennis, women's volleyball
$ Given: Unspecified number of awards ranging: $250-$6270 (full tuition)
Deadline: Contact the department coach
Contact: Mr. Mark Benedetto, Athletic Director

California Polytechnic State University, San Luis Obispo
San Luis Obispo, CA 93407
(805) 756-2923

Description: Athletic scholarships for undergraduates
Restrictions: Limited to scholarships for men's baseball, men's and women's basketball and cross country, men's football, women's softball, men's and women's track and field, women's volleyball, men's wrestling
$ Given: Unspecified number of awards ranging: $1,300-$3,300
Deadline: Contact the department coach
Contact: Mr. John McCutcheon, Athletic Director

California State Polytechnic University, Pomona
Pomona, CA 91768
(714) 869-2810

Description: Athletic scholarships for undergraduates
Restrictions: Limited to scholarships for men's baseball, men's and women's basketball and cross country, women's gymnastics, men's and women's soccer, women's softball, men's and women's tennis and track and field, women's volleyball
$ Given: 29 grants for men and women totaling $52,035
Deadline: Contact the department coach
Contact: Ms. Karen Miller, Athletic Director

California State University, Bakersfield
9001 Stockdale Highway
Bakersfield, CA 93311
(805) 664-3016

Description: Athletic scholarships for undergraduates
Restrictions: Limited to scholarships for men's basketball, men's and women's cross country, men's soccer, men's and women's swimming, tennis and track and field, women's volleyball, men's wrestling
$ Given: Unspecified number of awards ranging: $250-$10,678 (full tuition)
Deadline: Contact the department coach
Contact: Mr. Rudy Karvajal, Athletic Director

California State University, Dominguez Hills
Carson, CA 90747
(310) 516-3893

Description: Athletic scholarships for undergraduates
Restrictions: Limited to scholarships for men's baseball, men's and women's basketball, men's golf, men's and women's soccer, women's softball and volleyball
$ Given: 85 grants for men and women; average range: $100-$6,000 (full tuition)
Deadline: Contact the department coach
Contact: Mr. Louis Murdock, Acting Athletic Director

California State University, Fresno
Fresno, CA 93710
(209) 278-3178

Description: Athletic scholarships for undergraduates
Restrictions: Limited to scholarships for men's baseball, men's and women's basketball, men's cross country, football and golf, women's gymnastics, men's soccer, women's softball, men's and women's swimming and tennis, men's track and field, women's volleyball, men's wrestling
$ Given: 42 grants for men, 26 grants for women; average range: $200-$5,800 (full tuition)
Deadline: Contact the department coach
Contact: Dr. Gary Cunningham, Athletic Director

FREE MONEY FOR ATHLETIC SCHOLARSHIPS

• • • • • • • • • • • • • • • • • • • •

California State University, Fullerton
Fullerton, CA 92634
(714) 773-2677

Description: Athletic scholarships for undergraduates
Restrictions: Limited to scholarships for men's baseball, men's and women's basketball, cross country, fencing and gymnastics, men's soccer, women's softball, women's tennis, men's and women's track and field, women's volleyball, men's wrestling
$ Given: Unspecified number of awards ranging: $2,000-$8,000 (full tuition)
Deadline: Contact the department coach
Contact: Mr. Bill Shumard, Athletic Director

California State University, Long Beach
1250 Bellflower Boulevard
Long Beach, CA 90840
(310) 985-7976

Description: Athletic scholarships for undergraduates
Restrictions: Limited to scholarships for men's baseball, men's and women's basketball, cross country, football and golf, women's softball, men's and women's swimming, tennis and track and field, women's volleyball, men's water polo
$ Given: Unspecified number of awards ranging $200-$13,300 (full tuition)
Deadline: Contact the department coach
Contact: Mr. Dave O'Brien, Acting Athletic Director

California State University, Los Angeles
5151 State University Drive
Los Angeles, CA 90032
(213) 343-3084

Description: Athletic scholarships for undergraduates
Restrictions: Limited to scholarships for men's baseball, men's and women's basketball, cross country and diving, men's soccer, men's and women's swimming, swimming-diving, tennis and track and field, women's volleyball, men's water polo
$ Given: Unspecified number of awards
Deadline: Contact the department coach
Contact: Mr. Carroll Dunn, Athletic Director

• •

California State University, Northridge
Northridge, CA 91330
(818) 885-3208

Description: Athletic scholarships for undergraduates
Restrictions: Limited to scholarships for men's baseball, men's and women's basketball, cross country and diving, men's football and golf, women's gymnastics, men's soccer, women's softball, men's and women's swimming, swimming-diving, tennis, track and field and volleyball
$ Given: Unspecified number of awards ranging: $200-$1,5200
Deadline: Contact the department coach
Contact: Mr. Bob Hiegert, Athletic Director

California State University, Sacramento
Sacramento, CA 95819
(916) 278-6481

Description: Athletic scholarships for undergraduates
Restrictions: Limited to scholarships for men's baseball, men's and women's basketball, men's football, women's softball, men's and women's swimming, tennis and track and field, women's volleyball
$ Given: Unspecified number of awards ranging: $200-$7,380 (full tuition)
Deadline: Contact the department coach
Contact: Mr. Lee McElroy, Athletic Director

Christian Heritage College
2100 Greenfield Drive
El Cajon, CA 92019
(619) 441-2200

Description: Athletic scholarships for undergraduates
Restrictions: Limited to scholarships for men's basketball and soccer, women's volleyball
$ Given: 6 grants for men totaling, 9 grants for women; average range: $1,000-$9,000
Deadline: Contact the department coach
Contact: Mr. Paul Berry, Athletic Director

Fresno Pacific College
1717 South Chestnut Avenue
Fresno, CA 93702
(209) 453-2041

Description: Athletic scholarships for undergraduates
Restrictions: Limited to scholarships for men's and women's basketball and cross country, men's soccer, men's and women's track and field
$ Given: 17 grants for men, 5 grants for women; average range: $500-$9,300 (full tuition)
Deadline: Contact the department coach
Contact: Mr. John Moore, Athletic Director

FREE MONEY FOR ATHLETIC SCHOLARSHIPS

• •

Loyola Marymount University
Los Angeles, CA 90045
(310) 338-2765

Description: Athletic scholarships for undergraduates
Restrictions: Limited to scholarships for men's baseball, men's and women's basketball, men's golf, men's and women's volleyball
$ Given: Unspecified number of awards ranging: $500-$13,000 (full tuition)
Deadline: Contact the department coach
Contact: Mr. Brian Quinn, Athletic Director

Master's College
Newhall, CA 91322
(805) 259-3540

Description: Athletic scholarships for undergraduates
Restrictions: Limited to scholarships for men's baseball, men's and women's basketball and cross country, men's soccer, women's volleyball
$ Given: 9 grants for men totaling $38,630, 3 grants for women totaling $6,000
Deadline: Contact the department coach
Contact: Mr. Mel Hankinson, Athletic Director

Pepperdine University
Malibu, CA 90265
(310) 456-4150

Description: Athletic scholarships for undergraduates
Restrictions: Limited to scholarships for men's baseball, men's and women's basketball and golf, women's soccer and swimming and diving, men's and women's tennis and volleyball, men's water polo
$ Given: Unspecified number of awards ranging: $500-$24,000 (full tuition)
Deadline: Contact the department coach
Contact: Mr. Wayne Wright, Director of Athletics

Point Loma Nazarene College
San Diego, CA 92106
(619) 221-2340

Description: Athletic scholarships for undergraduates
Restrictions: Limited to scholarships for men's baseball, men's and women's basketball and cross country, men's golf and soccer, men's and women's tennis and track and field
$ Given: Unspecified number of awards
Deadline: Contact the department coach
Contact: Dr. Carroll Land, Director of Athletics

• • • • • • • • • • • • • • • • • • •

Saint Mary's College of California
Moraga, CA 94575
(510) 631-4000

Description: Athletic scholarships for undergraduates
Restrictions: Limited to scholarships for men's baseball, men's and women's basketball and cross country, men's football and golf, men's and women's soccer, women's softball, men's and women's tennis, women's volleyball
$ Given: Unspecified number of awards
Deadline: Contact the department coach
Contact: Mr. Rick Mauzzto, Athletic Director

San Diego State University
5300 Campanile Drive
San Diego, CA 92182
(619) 594-5163

Description: Athletic scholarships for undergraduates
Restrictions: Limited to scholarships for men's and women's basketball and cross country, men's football, men's and women's golf, women's gymnastics, men's soccer, men's and women's tennis, track and field and volleyball
$ Given: Unspecified number of awards
Deadline: Contact the department coach
Contact: Dr. Fred Miller, Athletic Director

San Jose State University
Washington Square
San Jose, CA 95192
(408) 924-1200

Description: Athletic scholarships for undergraduates
Restrictions: Limited to scholarships for men's baseball, men's and women's basketball, men's cross country, women's field hockey, men's football, men's and women's golf and gymnastics, men's soccer, women's softball and swimming, men's and women's tennis, men's track and field, women's volleyball, men's wrestling
$ Given: 24 grants for men totaling $50,250, 13 grants for women totaling $24,750 ('92-'93)
Deadline: Contact the department coach
Contact: Mr. Lawrence Fan, Sports Information Director

FREE MONEY FOR ATHLETIC SCHOLARSHIPS

. . . .

Santa Clara University
Santa Clara, CA 95053
(408) 554-4063

Description: Athletic scholarships for undergraduates
Restrictions: Limited to scholarships for men's baseball, men's and women's basketball, men's football, men's and women's soccer, women's volleyball
$ Given: 26 grants for men totaling $228,232, 10 grants for women totaling $85,441
Deadline: Contact the department coach
Contact: Mr. Carroll Williams, Director of Athletics

Southern California College
Costa Mesa, CA 92626
(714) 556-3610

Description: Athletic scholarships for undergraduates
Restrictions: Limited to scholarships for men's baseball, men's and women's basketball and cross country, men's soccer, women's softball and volleyball
$ Given: 16 grants for men, 11 grants for women; average range: $200-$12,500 (full tuition)
Deadline: Contact the department coach
Contact: Mr. Ron Pettyman, Director of Athletics

Stanford University
214 Old Union
Stanford, CA 94305
(415) 723-1543

Description: Athletic scholarships for undergraduates
Restrictions: Limited to scholarships for men's and women's basketball, cross country and fencing, women's field hockey, men's football, men's and women's golf and gymnastics, men's soccer, men's and women's swimming and diving, tennis, track and field and volleyball, men's water polo and wrestling
$ Given: 53 grants for men and women ('92-'93)
Deadline: Contact the department coach
Contact: Mr. Ted Leland, Director of Athletics

University of California at Berkeley
177 Hearst Gymnasium
Berkeley, CA 94720
(510) 642-0580

Description: Athletic scholarships for undergraduates
Restrictions: Limited to scholarships for men's and women's basketball, men's cross country, football, golf and gymnastics, men's and women's swimming and diving, tennis and track and field, men's water polo
$ Given: 45 grants for men totaling $450,000, 15 grants for women totaling $150,000
Deadline: Contact the department coach
Contact: Dr. Bob Backrath, Director of Athletics

· ·

University of California, Irvine
102 Administration Building
Irvine, CA 92717
(714) 856-6266

Description: Athletic scholarships for undergraduates
Restrictions: Limited to scholarships for men's and women's basketball and cross country, men's golf, men's and women's swimming and diving, tennis and track and field, women's volleyball, men's water polo
$ Given: 11 grants for men, 11 grants for women; average range: $1,000-$9,700 (full tuition)
Deadline: Contact the department coach
Contact: Mr. Dan Guerrero, Athletic Director

University of California, Los Angeles
405 Hilgard Avenue
Los Angeles, CA 90024-1435
(310) 825-8699

Description: Athletic scholarships for undergraduates
Restrictions: Limited to scholarships for men's and women's basketball and cross country, men's football, men's and women's golf and gymnastics, men's soccer, women's softball, men's and women's swimming and diving, tennis, track and field and volleyball, men's water polo
$ Given: 137 grants for men and women ('92-'93); average range: Up to $23,230 (full tuition)
Deadline: Contact the department coach
Contact: Mr. Pete Dalis, Director of Athletics

University of California, Riverside
Riverside, CA 92521
(714) 787-5432

Description: Athletic scholarships for undergraduates
Restrictions: Limited to scholarships for men's and women's basketball, men's cross country, tennis and track and field, women's volleyball
$ Given: Unspecified number of awards ranging: $250-$6,000
Deadline: Contact the department coach
Contact: Mr. John Masi, Director of Athletics

FREE MONEY FOR ATHLETIC SCHOLARSHIPS

• •

**University of California,
Santa Barbara**
Santa Barbara, CA 93106
(805) 893-3291

Description: Athletic scholarships for undergraduates
Restrictions: Limited to scholarships for men's baseball, men's and women's basketball, cross country, gymnastics and soccer, women's softball, men's and women's swimming and diving, tennis, track and field and volleyball, men's water polo
$ Given: 37 grants for men, 32 grants for women; average range: $250-$10,000 (full tuition)
Deadline: Contact the department coach
Contact: Mr. John Kasser, Athletic Director

University of San Diego
Alcala Park
San Diego, CA 92110
(619) 260-4803

Description: Athletic scholarships for undergraduates
Restrictions: Limited to scholarships for men's and women's basketball, women's swimming and diving, men's and women's tennis, women's volleyball
$ Given: Grants for men totaling $91,500, grants for women totaling $67,900; average range: Up to $12,000 (full tuition)
Deadline: Contact the department coach
Contact: Mr. Tom Iannacone, Athletic Director

**University of San
Francisco**
2130 Fulton Street
San Francisco, CA 94117
(415) 666-6891

Description: Athletic scholarships for undergraduates
Restrictions: Limited to scholarships for men's baseball, men's and women's basketball, golf and soccer, women's softball, men's and women's tennis, women's volleyball
$ Given: 28 grants for men and women; average range: Up to $19,152 (full tuition)
Deadline: Contact the department coach
Contact: Mr. Bill Hogan, Director of Athletics

• • • • • • • • • • • • • • • • • • • •

COLORADO

Adams State College
Stadium Drive
Alamosa, CO 81102
(719) 589-7011

Description: Athletic scholarships for undergraduates
Restrictions: Limited to scholarships for men's and women's basketball and cross country, men's football, men's and women's track and field, women's volleyball, men's wrestling
$ Given: 100 grants for men totaling $121,400, 60 grants for women totaling $72,840
Deadline: Contact the department coach
Contact: Ms. Vivian Frausto, Athletic Director

Colorado Christian University
180 Sputh Garrison
Lakewood, CO 80226
(303) 238-5386

Description: Athletic scholarships for undergraduates
Restrictions: Limited to scholarships for men's and women's basketball, men's golf, men's and women's soccer and tennis, women's volleyball
$ Given: Unspecified number of awards
Deadline: Contact the department coach
Contact: Mr. Frank Evans, Athletic Director

Colorado School of Mines
Golden, CO 80401
(303) 273-3360

Description: Athletic scholarships for undergraduates
Restrictions: Limited to scholarships for men's alpine skiing and baseball, men's and women's basketball, men's cross country, cross country skiing and football, men's and women's golf, men's lacrosse, women's softball, men's and women's swimming and diving, tennis, track and field, women's volleyball, men's wrestling
$ Given: 75 grants for men totaling $150,000, 35 grants for women totaling $70,000
Deadline: Contact the department coach
Contact: Mr. Bruce Allison, Director of Athletics

FREE MONEY FOR ATHLETIC SCHOLARSHIPS

• • • • • • • • • • • • • • • • • • • •

Colorado State University
Fort Collins, CO 80523
(303) 491-5300

Description: Athletic scholarships for undergraduates
Restrictions: Limited to scholarships for men's baseball, men's and women's basketball and cross country, men's football, women's softball and swimming and diving, men's and women's track and field, women's volleyball
$ Given: Unspecified number of awards
Deadline: Contact the department coach
Contact: Mr. Corey Johnson, Athletic Director

Fort Lewis College
Durango, CO 81301
(303) 247-7571

Description: Athletic scholarships for undergraduates
Restrictions: Limited to scholarships for men's and women's basketball and cross country, men's football, men's soccer, women's softball and volleyball, men's wrestling
$ Given: 29 grants for men totaling $24,500, 18 grants for women totaling $16,750; average range: $400-$2,000
Deadline: Contact the department coach
Contact: Mr. Bruce Grimes, Athletic Director

Mesa State College
1175 Texas
Grand Junction, CO 81501
(303) 248-1635

Description: Athletic scholarships for undergraduates
Restrictions: Limited to scholarships for men's and women's basketball, women's cross country, men's football, men's and women's tennis, women's volleyball
$ Given: 73 grants for men totaling $104,536, 27 grants for women totaling $38,664; average range: $500-$6,500 (full tuition)
Deadline: Contact the department coach
Contact: Mr. Jay Jefferson, Athletic Director

Metropolitan State College
1006 11th Street
Denver, CO 80217
(303) 556-8300

Description: Athletic scholarships for undergraduates
Restrictions: Limited to scholarships for men's and women's basketball, soccer, swimming and diving and tennis, women's volleyball
$ Given: Unspecified number of awards ranging: Up to $9,000 (full tuition)
Deadline: Contact the department coach
Contact: Mr. William Helman, Athletic Director

• • • • • • • • • • • • • • • • • • • •

Regis College
West 50th and Lowell
Boulevard
Denver, CO 80221
(303) 458-4070

Description: Athletic scholarships for undergraduates
Restrictions: Limited to scholarships for men's baseball, men's and women's basketball, men's and women's golf and soccer, women's softball, men's and women's tennis, women's volleyball
$ Given: 19 grants for men, 24 grants for women ('92-'93)
Deadline: Contact the department coach
Contact: Mr. Tom Dedin, Athletic Director

University of Colorado at Boulder
Boulder, CO 80309
(303) 492-7931

Description: Athletic scholarships for undergraduates
Restrictions: Limited to scholarships for men's and women's alpine skiing, basketball, cross country and cross country skiing, men's football and golf, men's and women's tennis and track and field, women's volleyball
$ Given: 32 grants for men, 13 grants for women ('92-'93); average range: Up to $11,000 (full tuition
Deadline: Contact the department coach
Contact: Mr. Bill Marolt, Athletic Director

University of Colorado at Colorado Springs
Colorado Springs, CO 80208
(719) 593-3000

Description: Athletic scholarships for undergraduates
Restrictions: Limited to scholarships for men's and women's basketball, men's golf and soccer, women's softball, men's and women's tennis, women's volleyball
$ Given: 6 grants for men, 15 grants for women ('92-'93)
Deadline: Contact the department coach
Contact: Mr. Theo Gregory, Athletic Director

University of Denver
Denver, CO 80208
(303) 871-2275

Description: Athletic scholarships for undergraduates
Restrictions: Limited to scholarships for men's baseball, men's and women's basketball, men's golf, women's gymnastics, men's ice hockey, men's and women's soccer, swimming and diving and tennis, women's volleyball
$ Given: 60 grants available totaling $534,000; average range: Up to $20,000 (full tuition)
Deadline: Contact the department coach
Contact: Mr. Jack McDonald, Athletic Director

FREE MONEY FOR ATHLETIC SCHOLARSHIPS

• •

University of Northern Colorado
Greeley, CO 90639
(303) 351-2534

Description: Athletic scholarships for undergraduates
Restrictions: Limited to scholarships for men's and women's basketball, women's soccer and swimming and diving, men's and women's tennis and track and field, women's volleyball, men's wrestling
$ Given: Unspecified number of awards
Deadline: Contact the department coach
Contact: Sue Jacobson, Acting Athletic Director

University of Southern Colorado
2200 North Bonforte Boulevard
Pueblo, CO 81001
(719) 549-2711

Description: Athletic scholarships for undergraduates
Restrictions: Limited to scholarships for men's and women's basketball, cross country, golf, tennis and track and field, women's volleyball, men's wrestling
$ Given: Unspecified number of awards ranging: Up to $10,000 (full tuition)
Deadline: Contact the department coach
Contact: Mr. Dan DeRose, Athletic Director

Western State College
Gunnison, CO 81230
(303) 943-2079

Description: Athletic scholarships for undergraduates
Restrictions: Limited to scholarships for men's and women's alpine skiing, basketball, cross country and cross country skiing, men's football, women's swimming-diving, men's and women's track and field, women's volleyball, men's wrestling
$ Given: Unspecified number of awards ranging: Up to $8,800 (full tuition)
Deadline: Contact the department coach
Contact: Mr. Kurt Mallory, Athletic Director

• • • • • • • • • • • • • • • • • • • •

CONNECTICUT

Central Connecticut State University
1615 Stanley Street
New Britain, CT 06050
(203) 827-7347

Description: Athletic scholarships for undergraduates
Restrictions: Limited to scholarships for men's and women's basketball and cross country, men's football, golf and soccer, women's softball, men's and women's swimming and diving, tennis and track and field, women's volleyball, men's wrestling
$ Given: 35 grants for men and women totaling $101,176
Deadline: Contact the department coach
Contact: Dr. Judith Davidson, Athletic Director

Quinnipiac College
New Road
Hamden, CT 06518
(203) 288-5251

Description: Athletic scholarships for undergraduates
Restrictions: Limited to scholarships for men's and women's basketball, cross country, soccer and tennis, women's volleyball
$ Given: 40 grants for men and women ('92-'93) ranging: Up to $18,000 (full tuition)
Deadline: Contact the department coach
Contact: Mr. Bert Kahn, Director of Athletics

University of Bridgeport
Bridgeport, CT 06601
(203) 576-4735

Description: Athletic scholarships for undergraduates
Restrictions: Limited to scholarships for men's and women's basketball, women's gymnastics, men's and women's soccer, women's softball, tennis and volleyball
$ Given: Unspecified number of awards ranging: $2,500-$18,500 (full tuition)
Deadline: Contact the department coach
Contact: Dr. Ann Farris, Athletic Director

FREE MONEY FOR ATHLETIC SCHOLARSHIPS

• • • • • • • • • • • • • • • • • • • •

University of Connecticut
U-78
2111 Hillside Road
Storrs, CT 06268
(203) 486-2000

Description: Athletic scholarships for undergraduates
Restrictions: Limited to scholarships for men's baseball, men's and women's basketball and cross country, women's field hockey, men's football and ice hockey, men's and women's soccer, women's softball, men's and women's swimming and diving and track and field, women's volleyball
$ Given: 35 grants for men, 19 grants for women ('92-'93); average range: Up to $16,288 (full tuition)
Deadline: Contact the department coach
Contact: Mr. Lew Turkins, Athletic Director

University of Hartford
200 Bloomfield Avenue
West Hartford, CT 06117
(203) 243-4658

Description: Athletic scholarships for undergraduates
Restrictions: Limited to scholarships for men's baseball, men's and women's basketball, cross country and golf, men's lacrosse, men's and women's soccer, women's softball, men's and women's tennis, women's volleyball, men's wrestling
$ Given: Unspecified number of awards ranging: $250-$22,500 (full tuition)
Deadline: Contact the department coach
Contact: Denise Cohen, Athletic Director

University of New Haven
300 Orange Avenue
West Haven, CT 06516
(203) 932-7022

Description: Athletic scholarships for undergraduates
Restrictions: Limited to scholarships for men's baseball, men's and women's basketball, men's cross country, football and soccer, women's softball and tennis, men's track and field, women's volleyball
$ Given: Unspecified number of awards ranging: $500-$15,300 (full tuition)
Deadline: Contact the department coach
Contact: Mr. William Leete, Athletic Director

DELAWARE

Delaware State College
Dupont Highway
Dover, DE 19901
(302) 739-4928

Description: Athletic scholarships for undergraduates
Restrictions: Limited to scholarships for men's and women's basketball and cross country, men's football, men's and women's track and field, men's wrestling
$ Given: Unspecified number of awards ranging: Up to $8,800 (full tuition)
Deadline: Contact the department coach
Contact: Mr. John Martin, Athletic Director

Goldey- Beacom College
Wilmington, DE 19808
(303) 998-8814

Description: Athletic scholarships for undergraduates
Restrictions: Limited to scholarships for men's soccer, women's softball
$ Given: Grants for men totaling $5,000, Grants for women totaling $5,000; average range: $50-$2,000
Deadline: Contact the department coach
Contact: Mr. Neal Isaac, Athletic Director

University of Delaware
Newark, DE 19716
(302) 451-2256

Description: Athletic scholarships for undergraduates
Restrictions: Limited to scholarships for men's baseball, men's and women's basketball, women's field hockey, men's football
$ Given: 20 grants for men, 8 grants for women ('92-'93)
Deadline: Contact the department coach
Contact: Mr. Edgar Johson, Athletic Director

Wilmington College
DuPont Highway
New Castle, DE 19720
(302) 328-9401

Description: Athletic scholarships for undergraduates
Restrictions: Limited to scholarships for men's baseball, men's and women's basketball, women's softball and volleyball
$ Given: Unspecified number of awards
Deadline: Contact the department coach
Contact: Mr. Craig Wolf or Mr. Jim Sherman, Directors of Athletics

• • • • • • • • • • • • • • • • • • • •

DISTRICT OF COLUMBIA

American University
Massachusetts and Ne-
braska Avenues, NW
Washington, DC 20016
(202) 885-3000

Description: Athletic scholarships for undergraduates
Restrictions: Limited to scholarships for men's basketball, women's field hockey, men's and women's soccer
and swimming and diving, women's tennis and volleyball,
men's wrestling
$ Given: Unspecified number of awards ranging: Up to
$23,100 (full tuition)
Deadline: Contact the department coach
Contact: Mr. Joe O'Donnell, Director of Athletics

Georgetown University
37th and O Street, NW
Washington, DC 20057
(202) 687-2435

Description: Athletic scholarships for undergraduates
Restrictions: Limited to scholarships for men's baseball,
men's and women's basketball and cross country, men's
lacrosse, men's and women's track and field, women's
volleyball
$ Given: Unspecified number of awards ranging: Up to
$23,607 (full tuition)
Deadline: Contact the department coach
Contact: Mr. Francis X. Rienzo, Director of the Athletic
Department

**George Washington
University**
600 22nd Street, NW
Washington, DC 20052
(202) 994-6650

Description: Athletic scholarships for undergraduates
Restrictions: Limited to scholarships for men's baseball,
men's and women's basketball, crew and cross country,
men's golf, women's gymnastics, men's and women's
soccer, swimming and diving and tennis, women's
volleyball
$ Given: 43 grants for men totaling $491,212, 33 grants
for women totaling $450,340 ('92-'93); average range: Up
to $24,000 (full tuition)
Deadline: Contact the department coach
Contact: Mr. Steve Bilsky, Director of Athletics

. . . .

Howard University
6th and Gerard Streets, NW
Washington, DC 20059
(202) 806-7140

Description: Athletic scholarships for undergraduates
Restrictions: Limited to scholarships for men's and women's basketball and cross country, men's soccer, men's and women's swimming and diving, tennis and track and field, women's volleyball, men's wrestling
$ Given: Unspecified number of awards
Deadline: Contact the department coach
Contact: Mr. David Simmons, Athletic Director

University of the District of Columbia
4200 Connecticut Avenue, NW
Washington, DC 20008
(202) 282-7748

Description: Athletic scholarships for undergraduates
Restrictions: Limited to scholarships for men's and women's basketball, men's football and soccer, men's and women's tennis and track and field, women's volleyball
$ Given: Unspecified number of awards ranging: $200-$8,000
Deadline: Contact the department coach
Contact: Mr. Dwight Datcher, Athletic Director

FLORIDA

Barry University
11300 N.E. 2nd Avenue
Miami Shores, FL 33161
(305) 899-3139

Description: Athletic scholarships for undergraduates
Restrictions: Limited to scholarships for men's baseball, men's and women's basketball and cross country, men's golf, men's and women's soccer, women's softball, men's and women's tennis, women's volleyball
$ Given: Unspecified number of awards ranging: $230-$10,500 (full tuition)
Deadline: Contact the department coach
Contact: Dr. Jean Cerra, Director of Athletics

Bethune-Cookman College
640 Second Avenue
Daytona Beach, FL 32015
(904) 255-1401

Description: Athletic scholarships for undergraduates
Restrictions: Limited to scholarships for men's and women's basketball, men's football
$ Given: 15 grants for men totaling $96,940, 2 grants for women totaling $15,244
Deadline: Contact the department coach
Contact: Mr. Lynn Thompson, Athletic Director

FREE MONEY FOR ATHLETIC SCHOLARSHIPS

• •

Eckerd College
5400 34th Street South
St. Petersburg, FL 33733
(813) 867-1166

Description: Athletic scholarships for undergraduates
Restrictions: Limited to scholarships for men's baseball, men's and women's basketball and cross country, men's golf and soccer, women's softball, men's and women's tennis, women's volleyball
$ Given: 35 grants for men totaling $157,500, 15 grants for women totaling $67,500; average range: $1,000-$5,000
Deadline: Contact the department coach
Contact: Mr. Jim Harley, Athletic Director

Florida Agricultural and Mechanical University
Martin Luther King Jr.
Boulevard
Tallahassee, FL 32307
(904) 599-3868

Description: Athletic scholarships for undergraduates
Restrictions: Limited to scholarships for men's and women's basketball and cross country, men's football, men's and women's golf, swimming and diving, tennis and track and field, women's volleyball
$ Given: Unspecified number of awards ranging: Up to $1,600 (full tuition)
Deadline: Contact the department coach
Contact: Dr. Walter Reed, Director of Athletics

Florida International University
Tamiami Trail
Miami, FL 33199
(305) 348-2756

Description: Athletic scholarships for undergraduates
Restrictions: Limited to scholarships for men's baseball, men's and women's basketball, crew, cross country, golf, soccer, tennis and track and field, women's volleyball
$ Given: Unspecified number of awards ranging: $250-$3,800 (full tuition)
Deadline: Contact the department coach
Contact: Mr. Ted Aceto, Athletic Director

Florida Memorial College
15800 N.W. 42nd Avenue
Miami, FL 33054
(305) 625-4141

Description: Athletic scholarships for undergraduates
Restrictions: Limited to scholarships for men's basketball, women's tennis
$ Given: Unspecified number of awards
Deadline: Contact the department coach
Contact: Mr. Alfred Parker, Athletic Director

• • • • • • • • • • • • • • • • • • • •

Florida Southern College
Lakeland, FL 33802
(813) 680-4244

Description: Athletic scholarships for undergraduates
Restrictions: Limited to scholarships for men's and women's basketball, men's golf and soccer, women's softball, tennis and volleyball
$ Given: Unspecified number of awards ranging: Up to $12,260 (full tuition)
Deadline: Contact the department coach
Contact: Mr. Hal Smeltzly, Director of Athletics

Florida State University
Tallahassee, FL 32306
(904) 644-1091

Description: Athletic scholarships for undergraduates
Restrictions: Limited to scholarships for men's baseball, men's and women's basketball and cross country, men's football, men's and women's golf, women's softball, men's and women's swimming and diving, tennis and track and field, women's volleyball
$ Given: Unspecified number of awards ranging: $500-$6,500 (full tuition)
Deadline: Contact the department coach
Contact: Mr. Bob Gorden, Director of Athletics

St. Thomas University
16400 NW 3rd Avenue
Miami, FL 33054
(305) 625-6000

Description: Athletic scholarships for undergraduates
Restrictions: Limited to scholarships for men's basketball and cross country, men's soccer, women's tennis
$ Given: Unspecified number of awards
Deadline: Contact the department coach
Contact: Dr. Andrew Kreutzer, Director of Athletics

University of Florida
Box 144485
Gainesville, FL 32604
(904) 375-4683

Description: Athletic scholarships for undergraduates
Restrictions: Limited to scholarships for men's baseball, men's and women's basketball and cross country, men's football, men's and women's golf, women's gymnastics, men's and women's swimming and diving, tennis and track and field, women's volleyball
$ Given: Unspecified number of awards ranging: Up to $10,156 (full tuition)
Deadline: Contact the department coach
Contact: Mr. Jeremy Foley, Athletic Director

FREE MONEY FOR ATHLETIC SCHOLARSHIPS

• •

University of Miami
Coral Gables, FL 33124
(305) 284-3822

Description: Athletic scholarships for undergraduates
Restrictions: Limited to scholarships for men's baseball, men's and women's basketball and diving, men's football, men's and women's golf, swimming and diving, tennis and track and field
$ Given: 44 grants for men and women; average range: $200-$23,000 (full tuition)
Deadline: Contact the department coach
Contact: Mr. Dave Maggard, Athletic Director

University of South Florida
4202 East Fowler Avenue
Tampa, FL 33620
(813) 974-2125

Description: Athletic scholarships for undergraduates
Restrictions: Limited to scholarships for men's baseball, men's and women's basketball and cross country, men's and women's golf, men's soccer, women's softball, men's and women's tennis and track and field, women's volleyball
$ Given: Unspecified number of awards ranging: Up to full tuition
Deadline: Contact the department coach
Contact: Mr. Paul Griffin, Director of Athletics

University of Tampa
401 West Kennedy Blvd.
Tampa, FL 33606
(813) 253-3333

Description: Athletic scholarships for undergraduates
Restrictions: Limited to scholarships for men's baseball, men's and women's basketball, men's golf and soccer, men's and women's swimming and diving, women's volleyball
$ Given: Unspecified number of awards
Deadline: Contact the department coach
Contact: Mr. Hindman Wall, Director of Athletics

. . . .

GEORGIA

Augusta College
2500 Walton Way
Augusta, GA 30910
(706) 737-1626

Description: Athletic scholarships for undergraduates
Restrictions: Limited to scholarships for men's and women's basketball and cross country, men's golf and soccer, women's swimming and diving, men's and women's tennis, men's volleyball
$ Given: Unspecified number of awards ranging: $200-$9,374 (full tuition)
Deadline: Contact the department coach
Contact: Mr. Clint Bryant, Athletic Director

Columbus College
Algonquin Drive
Columbus, GA 31993
(706) 568-2044

Description: Athletic scholarships for undergraduates
Restrictions: Limited to scholarships for men's basketball and golf, men's and women's tennis
$ Given: Unspecified number of awards ranging: $200-$8,000
Deadline: Contact the department coach
Contact: Mr. Herbert Greene, Athletic Director

Covenant College
Lookout Mountain, GA 30750
(706) 820-1560

Description: Athletic scholarships for undergraduates
Restrictions: Limited to scholarships for men's and women's basketball, men's soccer
$ Given: Unspecified number of awards
Deadline: Contact the department coach
Contact: Dr. Brian Crossman, Director of Athletics

Fort Valley State College
State College Drive
Fort Valley, GA 31030
(912) 825-6209

Description: Athletic scholarships for undergraduates
Restrictions: Limited to scholarships for men's and women's basketball, men's football, men's and women's tennis and track and field, women's volleyball
$ Given: Unspecified number of awards ranging: Up to $7,000 (full tuition)
Deadline: Contact the department coach
Contact: Mr. Douglas T. Porter, Athletic Director

FREE MONEY FOR ATHLETIC SCHOLARSHIPS

• • • • • • • • • • • • • • • • • • • •

Georgia College
Milledgeville, GA 31061
(912) 453-4072

Description: Athletic scholarships for undergraduates
Restrictions: Limited to scholarships for men's and women's basketball and golf, women's gymnastics, and softball, men's and women's tennis
$ Given: 14 grants for men totaling $19,719, 3 grants for women totaling $5,322
Deadline: Contact the department coach
Contact: Mr. Stan Aldridge, Athletic Director

Georgia Institute of Technology
190 Third Street, NW
Atlanta, GA 30332
(404) 894-5400

Description: Athletic scholarships for undergraduates
Restrictions: Limited to scholarships for men's baseball, men's and women's basketball and cross country, men's football and golf, women's softball, men's and women's swimming and diving, tennis and track and field, women's volleyball, men's wrestling
$ Given: Unspecified number of awards ranging: $100-$12,520 (full tuition)
Deadline: Contact the department coach
Contact: Mr. Homer Rice, Athletic Director

Georgia Southern University
Statesboro, GA 30460
(912) 681-5376

Description: Athletic scholarships for undergraduates
Restrictions: Limited to scholarships for men's baseball, men's and women's basketball and cross country, men's football, golf and soccer, women's softball, men's and women's swimming and diving and tennis
$ Given: Unspecified number of awards ranging: Up to $8,166 (full tuition)
Deadline: Contact the department coach
Contact: Dr. David Wagner, Athletic Director

Georgia Southwestern College
Wheatley Street
Americus, GA 31709
(912) 928-1262

Description: Athletic scholarships for undergraduates
Restrictions: Limited to scholarships for men's baseball, men's and women's basketball, men's golf, men's and women's tennis
$ Given: Unspecified number of awards ranging: $100-$3,600
Deadline: Contact the department coach
Contact: Dr. Bob C. Clark, Athletic Director

· ·

Georgia State University
University Plaza
Atlanta, GA 30303
(404) 651-2772

Description: Athletic scholarships for undergraduates
Restrictions: Limited to scholarships for men's baseball, men's and women's basketball, cross country and golf, men's soccer, women's softball, men's and women's tennis and track and field, women's volleyball, men's wrestling
$ Given: 7 grants for men, 13 grants for women ('92-'93); average range: $200-$6,500 (full tuition)
Deadline: Contact the department coach
Contact: Mr. Orby Moss, Athletic Director

Morehouse College
830 Westview Drive, SW
Atlanta, GA 30314
(404) 681-2800

Description: Athletic scholarships for undergraduates
Restrictions: Limited to scholarships for men's basketball, cross country, football, swimming and diving, tennis and track and field
$ Given: Unspecified number of awards ranging: Up to $13,224 (full tuition)
Deadline: Contact the department coach
Contact: Mr. Arthur McAfee, Athletic Director

Paine College
1235 15th Street
Augusta, GA 30910
(706) 821-8353

Description: Athletic scholarships for undergraduates
Restrictions: Limited to scholarships for men's and women's basketball, cross country and track and field, women's volleyball
$ Given: Unspecified number of awards ranging: $1,000-$8,500
Deadline: Contact the department coach
Contact: Mr. Ronny Spry, Athletic Director

Piedmont College
Demorest, GA 30535
(706) 778-3000

Description: Athletic scholarships for undergraduates
Restrictions: Limited to scholarships for men's baseball, men's and women's basketball, cross country, golf and soccer, women's softball, men's and women's tennis
$ Given: Grants for men totaling $64,000, grants for women totaling $45,000; average range: Up to $5,000
Deadline: Contact the department coach
Contact: Mr. Todd Brooks, Athletic Director

FREE MONEY FOR ATHLETIC SCHOLARSHIPS

University of Georgia
P.O. Box 1472
Athens, GA 30613
(706) 542-1306

Description: Athletic scholarships for undergraduates
Restrictions: Limited to scholarships for men's baseball, men's and women's basketball, cross country, men's football, men's and women's golf, women's gymnastics, men's and women's swimming and diving, tennis and track and field, women's volleyball
$ Given: Unspecified number of awards ranging: $200-$10,000 (full tuition)
Deadline: Contact the department coach
Contact: Mr. Vince Dooley, Athletic Director

Valdosta State College
Valdosta, GA 31613
(912) 333-5890

Description: Athletic scholarships for undergraduates
Restrictions: Limited to scholarships for men's baseball, men's and women's basketball, men's football, women's softball, men's and women's tennis
$ Given: 28 grants for men, 6 grants for women ('92-'93); average range: $50-$8,033 (full tuition)
Deadline: Contact the department coach
Contact: Mr. Herb Reinhard, Athletic Director

West Georgia College
Carrollton, GA 30118
(404) 836-6533

Description: Athletic scholarships for undergraduates
Restrictions: Limited to scholarships for men's and women's basketball and cross country, men's football and golf, men's and women's tennis, women's volleyball
$ Given: 22 grants for men, 13 grants for women; average range: $150-$4,650 (full tuition)
Deadline: Contact the department coach
Contact: Mr. David Dugan, Athletic Director

HAWAII

Brigham Young University - Hawaii Campus
Laie, HI 96762
(808) 293-3764

Description: Athletic scholarships for undergraduates
Restrictions: Limited to scholarships for men's basketball, men's and women's cross country and tennis, women's volleyball
$ Given: Unspecified number of awards ranging: Up to $6,530 (full tuition)
Deadline: Contact the department coach
Contact: Mr. Ken Wagner, Director of Athletics

Chaminade University of Honolulu
3140 Waialae Avenue
Honolulu, HI 96816-1578
(808) 735-4790

Description: Athletic scholarships for undergraduates
Restrictions: Limited to scholarships for men's baseball, women's volleyball
$ Given: Grants for men totaling $60,000, grants for women totaling $47,000
Deadline: Contact the department coach
Contact: Mr. Michael Vasconscellos, Athletic Director

Hawaii Pacific University
1060 Bishop Street, PH
Honolulu, HI 96813
(808) 544-0221

Description: Athletic scholarships for undergraduates
Restrictions: Limited to scholarships for men's baseball and basketball, men's and women's cross country, men's soccer, women's softball, men's and women's tennis, women's volleyball
$ Given: 12 grants for men totaling $24,561, 20 grants for women totaling $43,790
Deadline: Contact the department coach
Contact: Mr. Paul Smith, Athletic Director

FREE MONEY FOR ATHLETIC SCHOLARSHIPS

• •

IDAHO

Boise State University
1910 University Drive
Boise, ID 83725
(208) 385-1826

Description: Athletic scholarships for undergraduates
Restrictions: Limited to scholarships for men's and women's basketball and cross country, men's football and golf, women's gymnastics, men's and women's tennis and track and field, women's volleyball, men's wrestling
$ Given: Unspecified number of awards
Deadline: Contact the department coach
Contact: Mr. Gene Bleymaier, Athletic Director

Idaho State College
741 South 17th Street
Pocatello, ID 83209
(208) 236-2771

Description: Athletic scholarships for undergraduates
Restrictions: Limited to scholarships for men's and women's basketball and cross country, men's football, men's and women's tennis, men's and women's track and field, women's volleyball
$ Given: 57 grants for men totaling $256,500, 19 grants for women totaling $85,500
Deadline: Contact the department coach
Contact: Mr. Randy Hoffman, Director of Athletics

Lewis-Clark State College
8th Avenue and 6th Street
Lewiston, ID 83501
(208) 799-2224

Description: Athletic scholarships for undergraduates
Restrictions: Limited to scholarships for men's baseball, men's and women's basketball and tennis, women's volleyball
$ Given: 10 grants for men totaling $10,084, 9 grants for women totaling $6,824
Deadline: Contact the department coach
Contact: Mr. Gary Piccone, Athletic Director

Northwest Nazarene College
Nampa, ID 83651
(208) 467-8876

Description: Athletic scholarships for undergraduates
Restrictions: Limited to scholarships for men's baseball, men's and women's basketball, men's soccer, men's and women's track and field, women's volleyball
$ Given: Unspecified number of awards
Deadline: Contact the department coach
Contact: Mr. Eric Forseth, Athletic Director

University of Idaho
Moscow, ID 83843
(208) 855-0200

Description: Athletic scholarships for undergraduates
Restrictions: Limited to scholarships for men's and women's basketball and cross country, men's football, men's and women's golf, men's and women's tennis and track and field, women's volleyball
$ Given: Unspecified number of awards ranging: $125-$9,200 (full tuition)
Deadline: Contact the department coach
Contact: Mr. Pete Lyske, Athletic Director

ILLINOIS

Bradley University
1501 West Bradley Avenue
Peoria, IL 61625
(309) 676-7611

Description: Athletic scholarships for undergraduates
Restrictions: Limited to scholarships for men's and women's basketball and cross country, men's golf and swimming and diving, men's and women's tennis and track and field, women's volleyball
$ Given: Unspecified number of awards ranging: $500-$18,000 (full tuition)
Deadline: Contact the department coach
Contact: Mr. Ron Ferguson, Athletic Director

Chicago State University
95th and King Drive
Chicago, IL 60628
(312) 995-2295

Description: Athletic scholarships for undergraduates
Restrictions: Limited to scholarships for men's and women's basketball and cross country, men's golf, men's and women's swimming and diving and track and field, women's volleyball, men's wrestling
$ Given: Unspecified number of awards ranging: $250-$7,000 (full tuition)
Deadline: Contact the department coach
Contact: Mr. Al Avance, Athletic Director

FREE MONEY FOR ATHLETIC SCHOLARSHIPS

• • • • • • • • • • • • • • • • • • • •

Depaul University
1011 West Belden Avenue
Chicago, IL 60614
(312) 341-8010

Description: Athletic scholarships for undergraduates
Restrictions: Limited to scholarships for men's and women's basketball and cross country, men's golf, men's and women's riflery, men's soccer, women's softball, men's and women's tennis and track and field, women's volleyball
$ Given: Unspecified number of awards ranging: Up to $15,590 (full tuition)
Deadline: Contact the department coach
Contact: Mr. Bill Bradshaw, Athletic Director

Eastern Illinois University
Lantz Gym
Charleston, IL 61920
(217) 581-2319

Description: Athletic scholarships for undergraduates
Restrictions: Limited to scholarships for men's baseball, men's and women's basketball and cross country, men's football and soccer, women's softball and tennis, men's and women's track and field, women's volleyball, men's wrestling
$ Given: Unspecified number of awards ranging: $100-$5,480
Deadline: Contact the department coach
Contact: Mr. Michael Ryan, Athletic Director

Illinois Institute of Technology
3300 South Federal Street
Chicago, IL 60616
(312) 567-3296

Description: Athletic scholarships for undergraduates
Restrictions: Limited to scholarships for men's basketball, men's and women's swimming and diving and tennis, women's volleyball
$ Given: Unspecified number of awards ranging: $500-$18,290 (full tuition)
Deadline: Contact the department coach
Contact: Mr. Jim Darrah, Athletic Director

Illinois State University
Normal, IL 61761
(309) 438-3633

Description: Athletic scholarships for undergraduates
Restrictions: Limited to scholarships for men's baseball, men's and women's basketball and cross country, men's football, men's and women's golf, women's gymnastics, men's soccer, women's softball, men's and women's tennis and track and field, men's wrestling
$ Given: Unspecified number of awards ranging: Up to $10,078 (full tuition)
Deadline: Contact the department coach
Contact: Mr. Rick Greenspan, Athletic Director

Judson College
1151 North State Street
Elgin, IL 60123
(708) 695-2500

Description: Athletic scholarships for undergraduates
Restrictions: Limited to scholarships for men's and women's basketball, men's soccer and tennis, women's volleyball
$ Given: 22 grants for men, 20 grants for women ('92-'93)
Deadline: Contact the department coach
Contact: Mr. Steve Burke, Athletic Director

Loyola University Chicago
6525 North Sheridan Road
Chicago, IL 60626
(312) 274-3000

Description: Athletic scholarships for undergraduates
Restrictions: Limited to scholarships for men's and women's basketball and cross country, men's golf and soccer, women's softball, men's swimming and diving, men's and women's track and field, women's volleyball
$ Given: 25 grants for men and women; average range: $1,000-$16,000
Deadline: Contact the department coach
Contact: Mr. Chuck Schwarz, Athletic Director

McKendree College
701 College Road
Lebanon, IL 62254
(618) 537-4481

Description: Athletic scholarships for undergraduates
Restrictions: Limited to scholarships for men's and women's basketball and cross country, men's golf and soccer, women's softball and volleyball
$ Given: 13 grants for men totaling $15,500, 7 grants for women totaling $9,000; average range: $200-$10,250 (full tuition)
Deadline: Contact the department coach
Contact: Mr. Harry Statham, Athletic Director

FREE MONEY FOR ATHLETIC SCHOLARSHIPS

• •

Northeastern Illinois University
5500 North St. Louis Avenue
Chicago, IL 60625
(312) 583-4050

Description: Athletic scholarships for undergraduates
Restrictions: Limited to scholarships for men's baseball, men's and women's basketball and cross country, men's golf, women's softball, men's and women's swimming and diving and tennis, women's volleyball
$ Given: Unspecified number of awards
Deadline: Contact the department coach
Contact: Dr. Vivian Fuller, Athletic Director

Northern Illinois University
De Kalb, IL 60115
(815) 753-1000

Description: Athletic scholarships for undergraduates
Restrictions: Limited to scholarships for men's baseball, men's and women's basketball, women's field hockey, men's football, men's and women's golf, women's gymnastics, women's softball, men's soccer, men's and women's swimming and diving and tennis, women's volleyball, men's wrestling
$ Given: 58 grants for men, 28 grants for women ('92-'92)
Deadline: Contact the department coach
Contact: Mr. Gerald O'Dell, Athletic Director

Northwestern University
1501 Central Street
Evanston, IL 60201
(708) 491-3205

Description: Athletic scholarships for undergraduates
Restrictions: Limited to scholarships for men's baseball, men's and women's basketball, cross country, women's field hockey, men's football and golf, women's softball, men's and women's swimming and diving and tennis, women's volleyball, men's wrestling
$ Given: Unspecified number of awards ranging: $220-$22,088 (full tuition)
Deadline: Contact the department coach
Contact: Dr. William Foster, Director of Athletics

• • • • • • • • • • • • • • • • • • •

Southern Illinois University at Carbondale
Carbondale, IL 62901
(618) 453-5311

Description: Athletic scholarships for undergraduates
Restrictions: Limited to scholarships for men's baseball, men's and women's basketball and cross country, women's field hockey, men's football, men's and women's golf, men's softball, men's and women's swimming and diving, tennis and track and field, women's volleyball
$ Given: Unspecified number of awards ranging: $200-$8,678 (full tuition)
Deadline: Contact the department coach
Contact: Mr. Jim Hart, Athletic Director

Southern Illinois University at Edwardsville
Edwardsville, IL 62026
(618) 692-2871

Description: Athletic scholarships for undergraduates
Restrictions: Limited to scholarships for men's baseball, men's and women's basketball and cross country, men's golf, men's and women's soccer, men's and women's tennis and track and field, men's wrestling
$ Given: Grants for men and women totaling $51,100; average range: $1,575-$1700
Deadline: Contact the department coach
Contact: Ms. Cindy Jones, Athletic Director

University of Illinois at Chicago
Chicago, IL 60680
(312) 996-2772

Description: Athletic scholarships for undergraduates
Restrictions: Limited to scholarships for men's and women's basketball, cross country and gymnastics, men's ice hockey and soccer, women's softball, men's and women's swimming and diving and tennis, women's volleyball
$ Given: Unspecified number of awards ranging: Up to $10,000 (full tuition)
Deadline: Contact the department coach
Contact: Mr. Tom Russo, Athletic Director

• • • • • • • • • • • • • • • • • • • •

University of Illinois at Urbana-Champaign
Champaign, IL 61820
(217) 333-3630

Description: Athletic scholarships for undergraduates
Restrictions: Limited to scholarships for men's baseball, men's and women's basketball and cross country, men's fencing and football, men's and women's golf and gymnastics, women's softball, men's and women's swimming and diving, tennis and track and field, women's volleyball, men's wrestling
$ Given: Unspecified number of awards ranging: Up to $7,950 (full tuition)
Deadline: Contact the department coach
Contact: Mr. Ron Guenther, Athletic Director

Western Illinois University
Macomb, IL 61455
(309) 298-1190

Description: Athletic scholarships for undergraduates
Restrictions: Limited to scholarships for men's baseball, men's and women's basketball, women's cross country, men's football, golf and soccer, women's softball, men's and women's swimming and diving and tennis, men's and women's track and field, women's volleyball
$ Given: 20 grants for men totaling $37,493, 23 grants for women totaling $36,435; average range: Up to $5,000 (full tuition)
Deadline: Contact the department coach
Contact: Mr. Gil Peterson or Ms. Helen Smiley, Directors of Athletics

INDIANA

Ball State University
2000 University Avenue
Mucie, IN 47306
(317) 285-8225

Description: Athletic scholarships for undergraduates
Restrictions: Limited to scholarships for men's baseball, men's and women's basketball and cross country, women's field hockey, men's football and golf, women's gymnastics, men's and women's swimming and diving, tennis, track and field and volleyball
$ Given: Unspecified number of awards ranging: $200-$9,240 (full tuition)
Deadline: Contact the department coach
Contact: Mr. Don Purvis, Athletic Director

• • • • • • • • • • • • • • • • • • •

Bethel College
1001 West McKinley
Avenue
Mishawaka, IN 46545
(219) 259-8511

Description: Athletic scholarships for undergraduates
Restrictions: Limited to scholarships for men's baseball, men's and women's basketball, cross country and golf, men's soccer, women's softball, men's and women's tennis, women's volleyball
$ Given: Unspecified number of awards
Deadline: Contact the department coach
Contact: Mr. Michael Lightfoot, Athletic Director

Butler University
4600 Sunset Avenue
Indianapolis, IN 46208
(317) 283-9375

Description: Athletic scholarships for undergraduates
Restrictions: Limited to scholarships for men's baseball, men's and women's basketball and cross country, men's football, golf and soccer, women's softball, men's and women's swimming and diving, tennis and track and field, women's volleyball
$ Given: Unspecified number of awards ranging: $100-$16,500 (full tuition)
Deadline: Contact the department coach
Contact: Mr. John Parry, Director of Athletics

Grace College
200 Seminary Drive
Winona Lake, IN 46590
(219) 372-5217

Description: Athletic scholarships for undergraduates
Restrictions: Limited to scholarships for men's baseball, men's and women's basketball, men's golf and soccer, women's softball, men's tennis and track and field, women's volleyball
$ Given: Unspecified number of awards ranging: Up to $3,030
Deadline: Contact the department coach
Contact: Mr. Phil Dick, Athletic Director

Huntington College
2300 College Avenue
Huntington, IN 46750
(219) 356-6000

Description: Athletic scholarships for undergraduates
Restrictions: Limited to scholarships for men's baseball, men's and women's basketball, cross country, and golf, men's soccer, men's and women's tennis and track and field, women's volleyball
$ Given: 27 grants for men, 15 grants for women ('92-'93)
Deadline: Contact the department coach
Contact: Mr. Tom Kind, Athletic Director

FREE MONEY FOR ATHLETIC SCHOLARSHIPS

Indiana State University
Terre Haute, IN 47809
(812) 237-4040

Description: Athletic scholarships for undergraduates
Restrictions: Limited to scholarships for men's baseball, men's and women's basketball and cross country, men's football, women's softball, men's and women's tennis and track and field, women's volleyball
$ Given: 132 grants for men totaling $153,810, 82 grants for women totaling $103,086; average range: $200-$9,480
Deadline: Contact the department coach
Contact: Mr. Brian Saison, Athletic Director

Indiana University, Bloomington
Athletic Department
Assembly Hall
Bloomington, IN 47405
(812) 855-2238

Description: Athletic scholarships for undergraduates
Restrictions: Limited to scholarships for men's and women's basketball and cross country, men's football, men's and women's golf, men's soccer, men's and women's swimming and diving, tennis and track and field, women's volleyball, men's wrestling
$ Given: 47 grants for men, 21 grants for women ('92-'93)
Deadline: Contact the department coach
Contact: Mr. Clarence Doninger, Athletic Director

Marian College
3200 Cold Spring Road
Indianapolis, IN 46222
(317) 929-0291

Description: Athletic scholarships for undergraduates
Restrictions: Limited to scholarships for men's baseball, men's and women's basketball, cross country and golf, women's softball, men's and women's tennis and track and field, women's volleyball
$ Given: 28 grants for men, 17 grants for women
Deadline: Contact the department coach
Contact: Mr. John Grimes, Athletic Director

• • • • • • • • • • • • • • • • • • •

Purdue University
West Lafayette, IN 47907
(317) 494-3189

Description: Athletic scholarships for undergraduates
Restrictions: Limited to scholarships for men's baseball, men's and women's basketball and cross country, women's field hockey, men's football, men's and women's golf, men's soccer, men's and women's swimming and diving, tennis and track and field, women's volleyball, men's wrestling
$ Given: Unspecified number of awards
Deadline: Contact the department coach
Contact: Mr. Morgan Burke, Athletic Director

Saint Joseph's College
Rensselear, IN 47978
(219) 866-6163

Description: Athletic scholarships for undergraduates
Restrictions: Limited to scholarships for men's baseball, men's and women's basketball and cross country, men's football, men's and women's golf and soccer, women's softball, men's and women's tennis, men's track and field, women's volleyball
$ Given: 27 grants for men, 13 grants for women ('92-'93); average range: $2,000-14,500
Deadline: Contact the department coach
Contact: Mr. Kieth Freeman, Interim Athletic Director

Tri-State University
Angola, IN 46703
(219) 665-4100

Description: Athletic scholarships for undergraduates
Restrictions: Limited to scholarships for men's baseball, men's and women's basketball, men's cross country, men's and women's fencing, men's golf, men's and women's soccer, tennis and track and field, women's volleyball
$ Given: 66 grants for men, 22 grants for women
Deadline: Contact the department coach
Contact: Mr. Butch Percham, Athletic Director

FREE MONEY FOR ATHLETIC SCHOLARSHIPS

• •

University of Evansville
P.O. Box 329
Evansville, IN 47702
(812) 479-2237

Description: Athletic scholarships for undergraduates
Restrictions: Limited to scholarships for men's baseball, men's and women's basketball and cross country, men's golf and soccer, men's and women's swimming and diving and tennis, women's volleyball
$ Given: 29 grants for men, 29 grants for women ('92-'93); average range: Up to $15,300 (full tuition)
Deadline: Contact the department coach
Contact: Mr. James Byers, Athletic Director

University of Indianapolis
1400 East Hanna Avenue
Indianapolis, IN 46227
(317) 788-3246

Description: Athletic scholarships for undergraduates
Restrictions: Limited to scholarships for men's baseball, men's and women's basketball and cross country, men's football, men's and women's golf, men's soccer, women's softball, men's and women's swimming and diving, tennis and track and field, women's volleyball, men's wrestling
$ Given: 63 grants for men, 26 grants for women ('92-'93); average range: $500-14,510 (full tuition)
Deadline: Contact the department coach
Contact: Mr. Bill Bright, Athletic Director

University of Notre Dame
Notre Dame, IN 46556
(219) 631-6107

Description: Athletic scholarships for undergraduates
Restrictions: Limited to scholarships for men's baseball, men's and women's basketball, men's cross country, men's and women's fencing, men's football, men's and women's golf, men's ice hockey, men's and women's soccer, women's softball, men's and women's swimming, swimming-diving, tennis and track and field, women's volleyball, men's wrestling
$ Given: 59 grants for men totaling $768,526, 31 grants for women totaling $276,173; average range: Up to $20,700 (full tuition)
Deadline: Contact the department coach
Contact: Mr. Richard Rosenthal, Athletic Director

• • • • • • • • • • • • • • • • • • • •

University of Southern Indiana
8600 University Boulevard
Evansville, IN 47712
(812) 464-1846

Description: Athletic scholarships for undergraduates
Restrictions: Limited to scholarships for men's baseball, men's and women's basketball and cross country, men's golf and soccer, women's softball, men's and women's tennis, women's volleyball
$ Given: 17 grants for men, 15 grants for women; average range: Up to $9,000 (full tuition)
Deadline: Contact the department coach
Contact: Dr. Donald Bennett, Athletic Director

Valparaiso University
Valparaiso, IN 46383
(219) 464-5230

Description: Athletic scholarships for undergraduates
Restrictions: Limited to scholarships for men's baseball, men's and women's basketball and cross country, men's football and golf, women's gymnastics, men's soccer, women's softball, men's and women's swimming and diving and tennis, women's volleyball, men's wrestling
$ Given: Unspecified number of awards ranging; $100-$15,260 (full tuition)
Deadline: Contact the department coach
Contact: Mr. William Steinbrecher, Athletic Director

IOWA

Briar Cliff College
3303 Rebecca Street
Sioux City, IA 51104
(712) 279-1656

Description: Athletic scholarships for undergraduates
Restrictions: Limited to scholarships for men's baseball, men's and women's basketball and golf, men's soccer, women's softball and volleyball
$ Given: 28 grants for men, 28 grants for women; average range: $500-$13,674 (full tuition)
Deadline: Contact the department coach
Contact: Mr. Mike Krozier, Athletic Director

FREE MONEY FOR ATHLETIC SCHOLARSHIPS

• • • • • • • • • • • • • • • • • • • •

Drake University
25th and University
Des Moines, IA 50311
(515) 271-2889

Description: Athletic scholarships for undergraduates
Restrictions: Limited to scholarships for men's and women's basketball and cross country, men's golf and soccer, women's softball, men's and women's tennis and track and field, women's volleyball, men's wrestling
$ Given: Unspecified number of awards ranging: Up to $17,000 (full tuition)
Deadline: Contact the department coach
Contact: Lynn King, Athletic Director

Graceland College
700 College Avenue
Lamoni, IA 50140
(515) 784-5311

Description: Athletic scholarships for undergraduates
Restrictions: Limited to scholarships for men's baseball, men's and women's basketball and cross country, men's football and golf, men's and women's soccer, women's softball, men's and women's tennis, track and field and volleyball
$ Given: 77 grants for men and women ('92-'93); full tuition not offered
Deadline: Contact the department coach
Contact: Mr. Tom Powell, Athletic Director

Grand View College
1200 Grand View
Des Moines, IA 50316
(515) 263-2897

Description: Athletic scholarships for undergraduates
Restrictions: Limited to scholarships for men's baseball, men's and women's basketball, cross country and golf, men's soccer, women's softball, men's and women's tennis, women's volleyball
$ Given: 19 grants for men, 7 grant for women ('92-'93); average range: Up to $13,500 (full tuition)
Deadline: Contact the department coach
Contact: Mr. Lou Yacinich, Athletic Director

Iowa State University of Science and Technology
Ames, IA 50011
(515) 294-3662

Description: Athletic scholarships for undergraduates
Restrictions: Limited to scholarships for men's baseball, men's and women's basketball and cross country, men's football, men's and women's golf and gymnastics, women's softball, men's and women's swimming and diving, tennis and track and field, women's volleyball, men's wrestling
$ Given: Unspecified number of awards ranging: $200-$10,816
Deadline: Contact the department coach
Contact: Mr. Max Urich, Athletic Director

Iowa Wesleyan College
Mount Pleasant, IA 52641
(319) 385-8021

Description: Athletic scholarships for undergraduates
Restrictions: Limited to scholarships for men's baseball, men's and women's basketball and cross country, men's football and golf, women's softball, men's and women's track and field, women's volleyball
$ Given: 39 grants for men, 17 grants for women ('92-'93)
Deadline: Contact the department coach
Contact: Mr. David Johnson, Athletic Director

Morningside College
1501 Morningside Avenue
Sioux City, IA 51106
(712) 274-5192

Description: Athletic scholarships for undergraduates
Restrictions: Limited to scholarships for men's baseball, men's and women's baseball and basketball, men's cross country and football, men's track and field, women's volleyball
$ Given: 13 grants for men, 9 grants for women ('92-'93); average range: Up to $13,896 (full tuition)
Deadline: Contact the department coach
Contact: Mr. Jerry Schmutte or Joan McDermott, Athletic Directors

FREE MONEY FOR ATHLETIC SCHOLARSHIPS

• •

Northwestern College
101 Seventh Street, SW
Orange City, IA 51041
(712) 737-4821

Description: Athletic scholarships for undergraduates
Restrictions: Limited to scholarships for men's baseball, men's and women's basketball and cross country, men's football, men's and women's golf, women's softball, men's and women's tennis, track and field and volleyball, men's wrestling
$ Given: 67 grants for men, 31 grants for women ('92-'93); average range $400-$4,800
Deadline: Contact the department coach
Contact: Mr. Todd Berry, Athletic Director

St. Ambrose University
518 West Locust Street
Davenport, IA 52803
(319) 383-8727

Description: Athletic scholarships for undergraduates
Restrictions: Limited to scholarships for men's baseball, men's and women's basketball and cross country, men's football, men's and women's golf, men's soccer, men's and women's tennis and track and field, women's volleyball
$ Given: 40 grants for men and women ('92-'93); average range: Up to $5,000
Deadline: Contact the department coach
Contact: Mr. Jim Fox, Athletic Director

University of Northern Iowa
23rd and College
Cedar Falls, IA 50614
(319) 273-2470

Description: Athletic scholarships for undergraduates
Restrictions: Limited to scholarships for men's baseball, men's and women's basketball and cross country, men's football, men's and women's golf, women's softball, swimming and diving and tennis, men's and women's track and field, women's volleyball, men's wrestling
$ Given: 41 grants for men, 18 grants for women ('92-'93); average range: Up to $8,542 (full tuition)
Deadline: Contact the department coach
Contact: Mr. Chris Ritrievi, Athletic Director

• • • • • • • • • • • • • • • • • • • •

KANSAS

Baker University
Baldwin City, KS 66006
(913) 594-6451

Description: Athletic scholarships for undergraduates
Restrictions: Limited to scholarships for men's baseball, men's and women's basketball and cross country, men's football and golf, men's and women's soccer, women's softball, men's and women's tennis and track and field, women's volleyball
$ Given: 81 grants for men, 38 grants for women
Deadline: Contact the department coach
Contact: Mr. Charlie Richards, Athletic Director

Benedictine College
Atchison, KS 66002
(913) 367-5340

Description: Athletic scholarships for undergraduates
Restrictions: Limited to scholarships for men's and women's basketball, men's football, men's and women's soccer, women's softball and volleyball
$ Given: Unspecified number of awards; average range $2,250-$4,500
Deadline: Contact the department coach
Contact: Mr. Larry Wilcox, Athletic Director

Bethany College
Lindsborg, KS 67117
(316) 283-2500

Description: Athletic scholarships for undergraduates
Restrictions: Limited to scholarships for men's and women's basketball and cross country, men's football, men's and women's golf, women's softball, men's and women's tennis and track and field
$ Given: 77 grants for men, 17 grants for women; average range: $500-$2,000
Deadline: Contact the department coach
Contact: Mr. George Stephens, Athletic Director

FREE MONEY FOR ATHLETIC SCHOLARSHIPS

• •

Emporia State University
Emporia, KS 66801
(316) 343-1200

Description: Athletic scholarships for undergraduates
Restrictions: Limited to scholarships for men's and women's basketball, bowling and cross country, men's football, men's and women's golf, men's and women's tennis and track and field, women's volleyball
$ Given: 33 grants for men totaling $72,704, 9 grants for women totaling $16,278
Deadline: Contact the department coach
Contact: Dr. William Quayle, Director of Athletics

Fort Hays State University
Hays, KS 67601
(913) 628-4050

Description: Athletic scholarships for undergraduates
Restrictions: Limited to scholarships for men's baseball, men's and women's basketball and cross country, men's football, men's and women's tennis and track and field, women's volleyball, men's wrestling
$ Given: Unspecified number of awards ranging: $100-$5,100 (full tuition)
Deadline: Contact the department coach
Contact: Mr. Tom Spicer, Athletic Director

Friends University
2100 University
Wichita, KS 67213
(316) 264-9627

Description: Athletic scholarships for undergraduates
Restrictions: Limited to scholarships for men's and women's basketball, men's football and golf, men's and women's soccer and tennis, women's volleyball
$ Given: Unspecified number of awards ranging: Up to $3,250
Deadline: Contact the department coach
Contact: Mr. Ron Heller, Athletic Director

Kansas Newman College
3100 McCormick Avenue
Wichita, KS 67213
(316) 942-4291, ext. 119

Description: Athletic scholarships for undergraduates
Restrictions: Limited to scholarships for men's baseball, women's basketball, men's golf, men's and women's soccer
$ Given: 7 grants for men, 7 grants for women
Deadline: Contact the department coach
Contact: Mr. Paul Sanagorski, Athletic Director

Kansas Wesleyan University
100 East Claflin
Salina, KS 67401-6196
(913) 827-5541

Description: Athletic scholarships for undergraduates
Restrictions: Limited to scholarships for men's baseball, men's and women's basketball and cross country, men's football, men's and women's golf, women's softball, men's and women's track and field, women's volleyball
$ Given: Unspecified number of awards ranging: $500-$4,000
Deadline: Contact the department coach
Contact: Ms. Glenna Alexander, Director of Financial Assistance

McPherson College
1600 East Euclid
McPherson, KS 67460
(316) 241-0731

Description: Athletic scholarships for undergraduates
Restrictions: Limited to scholarships for men's and women's basketball and cross country, men's football, men's and women's golf, tennis and track and field, women's volleyball
$ Given: 15 grants for men, 14 grants for women ('92-'93); average range: $500-$1,500
Deadline: Contact the department coach
Contact: Mr. Dan Hoffman, Athletic Director

Pittsburg State University
Pittsburg, KS 66762
(316) 231-7000

Description: Athletic scholarships for undergraduates
Restrictions: Limited to scholarships for men's baseball, men's and women's basketball, men's cross country, men's football, women's softball, men's and women's track and field, women's volleyball
$ Given: 9 grants for men, 10 grants for women ('92-'93); average range: Up to $4,500 (full tuition)
Deadline: Contact the department coach
Contact: Mr. Bill Samuels, Athletic Director

FREE MONEY FOR ATHLETIC SCHOLARSHIPS

• •

Southwestern College
North College
Winfield, KS 67156
(316) 221-4150

Description: Athletic scholarships for undergraduates
Restrictions: Limited to scholarships for men's and women's basketball and cross country, men's football and golf, men's and women's tennis and track and field, women's volleyball
$ Given: 61 grants for men, 9 grants for women ('92-'93); average range: Up to $3,000
Deadline: Contact the department coach
Contact: Mr. Jim Helmer, Acting Director of Athletics

Tabor College
400 East Jefferson
Hillsboro, KS 67063
(316) 947-3121

Description: Athletic scholarships for undergraduates
Restrictions: Limited to scholarships for men's and women's basketball, men's football and soccer, men's and women's tennis, women's volleyball
$ Given: 80 grants for men and women ('92-'93); average range: $1,000-$1,500
Deadline: Contact the department coach
Contact: Mr. Gary Myers, Athletic Director

University of Kansas
Allen Fieldhouse
Lawrence, KS 66045
(913) 864-3143

Description: Athletic scholarships for undergraduates
Restrictions: Limited to scholarships for men's baseball, men's and women's basketball and cross country, men's football, men's and women's golf, women's softball, men's and women's swimming and diving, tennis and track and field, women's volleyball
$ Given: 222 grants for men, 113 grants for women ('92-'93); average range: Up to $6,818 (full tuition)
Deadline: Contact the department coach
Contact: Mr. Bob Frederick, Athletic Director

Wichita State University
Wichita, KS 67208
(316) 689-3250

Description: Athletic scholarships for undergraduates
Restrictions: Limited to scholarships for men's baseball, men's and women's basketball and cross country, men's and women's golf, women's softball, men's and women's tennis and track and field, women's volleyball
$ Given: Unspecified number of awards ranging: $200-$10,000 (full tuition)
Deadline: Contact the department coach
Contact: Mr. Gary Hunter, Athletic Director

KENTUCKY

Alice Lloyd College
Pippa Passes, KY 41844
(606) 368-2101

Description: Athletic scholarships for undergraduates
Restrictions: Limited to scholarships for men's baseball and men's and women's basketball and cross country
$ Given: 5 grants for men totaling $34,000, 5 grants for women totaling $41,000 ('92-'93)
Deadline: Contact the department coach
Contact: Mr. Jim Stept, Athletic Director

Bellarmine College
Newburg Road
Louisville, KY 40205
(502) 452-8381

Description: Athletic scholarships for undergraduates
Restrictions: Limited to scholarships for men's baseball, men's and women's basketball and cross country, women's field hockey, men's golf, men's and women's soccer, women's softball, men's and women's tennis and track and field, women's volleyball
$ Given: Grants for men totaling $39,830, grants for women totaling $51,690; average range: $500-$10,730 (full tuition)
Deadline: Contact the department coach
Contact: Mr. James R. Spalding, Athletic Director

Brescia College
120 West 7th Street
Owensboro, KY 42301
(502) 685-1674

Description: Athletic scholarships for undergraduates
Restrictions: Limited to scholarships for men's and women's basketball, men's golf and soccer, women's volleyball
$ Given: Unspecified number of awards
Deadline: Contact the department coach
Contact: Athletic department Director

57

FREE MONEY FOR ATHLETIC SCHOLARSHIPS

• •

Cumberland College
Williamsburg, KY 40769
(606) 549-2200

Description: Athletic scholarships for undergraduates
Restrictions: Limited to scholarships for men's baseball, men's and women's basketball, men's cross country and golf, women's softball, men's and women's tennis
$ Given: Unspecified number of awards
Deadline: Contact the department coach
Contact: Mr. Henry Morgan, Athletic Director

Eastern Kentucky University
Lancaster Avenue
Richmond, KY 40475
(606) 622-3654

Description: Athletic scholarships for undergraduates
Restrictions: Limited to scholarships for men's baseball, men's and women's basketball and cross country, men's football and golf, women's softball, men's and women's tennis and track and field, women's volleyball
$ Given: Unspecified number of awards ranging: Up to $8,100 (full tuition)
Deadline: Contact the department coach
Contact: Mr. Roy Kidd, Athletic Director

Georgetown College
Georgetown, KY 40324
(502) 863-8115

Description: Athletic scholarships for undergraduates
Restrictions: Limited to scholarships for men's baseball, men's and women's basketball and cross country, men's golf and soccer, women's softball, men's and women's tennis, women's volleyball
$ Given: Unspecified number of grants
Deadline: Contact the department coach
Contact: Mr. James Reid, Athletic Director

Kentucky State University
East Main Street
Frankfurt, KY 40601
(502) 227-6000

Description: Athletic scholarships for undergraduates
Restrictions: Limited to scholarships for men's and women's basketball and cross country, men's football, men's and women's golf, tennis and track and field, women's volleyball
$ Given: 48 grants for men, 28 grants for women ('92-'93); average range: $1,000-$7,000 (full tuition)
Deadline: Contact the department coach
Contact: Mr. D.W. Lyons, Athletic Director

• • • • • • • • • • • • • • • • • • • •

Kentucky Wesleyan College
3000 Fredrich
Owensboro, KY 42301
(502) 683-4795

Description: Athletic scholarships for undergraduates
Restrictions: Limited to scholarships for men's baseball, men's and women's basketball, men's cross country, golf and soccer, women's tennis and volleyball
$ Given: Grants for men and women totaling $63,147
Deadline: Contact the department coach
Contact: Mr. Wayne Boultinghouse, Athletic Director

Morehead State University
Morehead, KY 40351
(606) 783-5136

Description: Athletic scholarships for undergraduates
Restrictions: Limited to scholarships for men's baseball, men's and women's basketball, men's football and golf, men's and women's tennis, women's volleyball
$ Given: 36 grants for men totaling $130,000, 14 grants for women totaling $59,045
Deadline: Contact the department coach
Contact: Mr. James Wells, Compliance Coordinator

Murray State University
Murray, KY 42071
(502) 762-6184

Description: Athletic scholarships for undergraduates
Restrictions: Limited to scholarships for men's and women's basketball and cross country, men's football and golf, men's and women's riflery, tennis and track and field, women's volleyball
$ Given: Unspecified number of awards
Deadline: Contact the department coach
Contact: Mr. Michael Stricland, Athletic Director

Transylvania University
300 North Broadway
Lexington, KY 40508
(606) 233-8270

Description: Athletic scholarships for undergraduates
Restrictions: Limited to scholarships for men's and women's basketball, men's golf and soccer, women's softball, men's and women's swimming and diving and tennis
$ Given: 12 grants for men totaling $58,924, 18 grants for women totaling $32,100 ('92-'93)
Deadline: Contact the department coach
Contact: Mr. Don Lane, Athletic Director

• •

Union College
Barbourville, KY 40906
(606) 546-4151

Description: Athletic scholarships for undergraduates
Restrictions: Limited to scholarships for men's baseball, men's and women's basketball, men's soccer, women's softball, men's and women's swimming and diving and tennis, women's volleyball
$ Given: 21 grants for men, 8 grants for women ('92-'93); average range: $200-$9,790
Deadline: Contact the department coach
Contact: Mr. Gary Sharpe, Athletic Director

University of Kentucky
Memorial Coliseum
Lexington, KY 40506-0019
(606) 257-3838

Description: Athletic scholarships for undergraduates
Restrictions: Limited to scholarships for men's baseball, men's and women's basketball and cross country, men's football, men's and women's golf, women's gymnastics, men's and women's swimming and diving, tennis, and track and field, women's volleyball
$ Given: Unspecified number of awards
Deadline: Contact the department coach
Contact: Mr. C.M. Newton, Athletic Director

University of Kentucky
Louisville, KY 40292
(502) 588-5732

Description: Athletic scholarships for undergraduates
Restrictions: Limited to scholarships for men's baseball, men's and women's basketball and cross country, men's football and golf and soccer, men's and women's swimming and diving, tennis and track and field, women's volleyball
$ Given: Unspecified number of awards ranging: Up to $9,500 (full tuition)
Deadline: Contact the department coach
Contact: Mr. William C. Olsen, Athletic Director

• •

Western Kentucky University
College Heights
Bowling Green, KY 42101
(502) 745-3542

Description: Athletic scholarships for undergraduates
Restrictions: Limited to scholarships for men's baseball, men's and women's basketball and cross country, men's football, men's and women's golf, men's swimming and diving, men's and women's tennis and track and field
$ Given: 85 grants for men, 23 grants for women ('92-'93); average range: $100-$7,644 (full tuition)
Deadline: Contact the department coach
Contact: Mr. Lou Marciani, Athletic Director

LOUISIANA

Grambling State University
Grambling, LA 71245
(318) 274-2000

Description: Athletic scholarships for undergraduates
Restrictions: Limited to scholarships for men's baseball, men's and women's basketball, men's football and golf, women's softball, men's and women's tennis and track and field
$ Given: Unspecified number of awards
Deadline: Contact the department coach
Contact: Mr. Fred Hobdy, Athletic Director

Louisiana College
Pineville, LA 71350
(318) 487-7386

Description: Athletic scholarships for undergraduates
Restrictions: Limited to scholarships for men's baseball, men's and women's basketball
$ Given: 24 grants for men, 24 grants for women; average range: Up to $9,000 (full tuition)
Deadline: Contact the department coach
Contact: Mr. Billy Allgood, Athletic Director

FREE MONEY FOR ATHLETIC SCHOLARSHIPS

• •

Louisiana State University and Agricultural and Mechanical College
P.O. Box 93008
Baton Rouge, LA 70803
(504) 388-2187

Description: Athletic scholarships for undergraduates
Restrictions: Limited to scholarships for men's baseball, men's and women's basketball and cross country, men's football, men's and women's golf, women's gymnastics, men's and women's swimming and diving, tennis, and track and field
$ Given: Unspecified number of awards ranging: Up to $9,572 (full tuition)
Deadline: Contact the department coach
Contact: Mr. Joe Dean, Athletic Director

Louisiana Tech University
Ruston, LA 71272
(318) 257-4111

Description: Athletic scholarships for undergraduates
Restrictions: Limited to scholarships for men's baseball, men's and women's basketball, men's cross country and football, women's softball and tennis, men's track and field
$ Given: Unspecified number of awards ranging: Up to $4,700 (full tuition)
Deadline: Contact the department coach
Contact: Mr. Jerry Stoball, Director of Athletics

McNesse State University
Ryan Street
Lake Charles, LA 70609
(318) 475-5140

Description: Athletic scholarships for undergraduates
Restrictions: Limited to scholarships for men's baseball, men's and women's basketball and cross country, men's football and golf, women's softball, men's and women's tennis and track and field, women's volleyball
$ Given: Unspecified number of awards ranging: $200-$5,400
Deadline: Contact the department coach
Contact: Mr. Bob Hayes, Athletic Director

Nicholls State University
P.O. Box 2032
Thibodaux, LA 70301
(504) 446-8111

Description: Athletic scholarships for undergraduates
Restrictions: Contact the athletic department director
$ Given: 174 grants for men, 51 grants for women; average range: Up to $4,500 (full tuition)
Deadline: Contact the department coach
Contact: Mr. Phil Greco, Athletic Director

. . . .

Northeast Louisiana University
700 University Avenue
Monroe, LA 71209
(318) 342-5321

Description: Athletic scholarships for undergraduates
Restrictions: Limited to scholarships for men's baseball, men's and women's basketball and cross country, men's football and golf, women's softball, men's and women's swimming, tennis and track and field, women's volleyball
$ Given: Unspecified number of awards ranging: $200-$6,291 (full tuition)
Deadline: Contact the department coach
Contact: Mr. Benny Hollis, Director of Athletics

Southeastern Louisiana University
North Hazel Street
Hammond, LA 70402
(504) 549-2253

Description: Athletic scholarships for undergraduates
Restrictions: Limited to scholarships for men's baseball, men's and women's basketball, men's cross country and golf, men's and women's tennis, women's volleyball
$ Given: Unspecified number of awards ranging: $250-$5,667 (full tuition)
Deadline: Contact the department coach
Contact: Mr. Tom Douple, Athletic Director

Southern University and Agricultural and Mechanical College
Baton Rouge, LA 70813
(504) 771-3170

Description: Athletic scholarships for undergraduates
Restrictions: Limited to scholarships for men's baseball, men's and women's basketball and cross country, men's football, golf and tennis, men's and women's track and field, women's volleyball
$ Given: Unspecified number of awards ranging: $4,145-$5,670
Deadline: Contact the department coach
Contact: Mr. Marino Casem, Athletic Director

Tulane University
Monk Simmons Building
New Orleans, LA 70118
(504) 865-5501

Description: Athletic scholarships for undergraduates
Restrictions: Limited to scholarships for men's baseball, women's basketball, men's and women's cross country, men's football and golf, men's and women's swimming and diving, tennis and track and field, women's volleyball
$ Given: 123 grants for men and women totaling $668,380; average range: Up to $23,975 (full tuition)
Deadline: Contact the department coach
Contact: Dr. Kevin White, Athletic Director

• • • • • • • • • • • • • • • • • • • •

University of New Orleans
Lake Front
New Orleans, LA 70148
(504) 286-6239

Description: Athletic scholarships for undergraduates
Restrictions: Limited to scholarships for men's baseball, men's and women's basketball, men's cross country, golf and soccer, women's swimming and diving, men's and women's tennis, men's track and field, women's volleyball
$ Given: Unspecified number of awards ranging: $500-$9,000 (full tuition)
Deadline: Contact the department coach
Contact: Mr. Ronald Maestri, Director of Athletics

MAINE

Husson College
One College Circle
Bangor, ME 04401
(207) 947-1121

Description: Athletic scholarships for undergraduates
Restrictions: Limited to scholarships for men's and women's basketball, men's golf, men's and women's soccer
$ Given: 34 grants for men, 21 grants for women ('92-'93)
Deadline: Contact the department coach
Contact: Ms. Pamela Hennessey, Athletic Director

Unity College
Unity, ME 04988
(207) 948-3131

Description: Athletic scholarships for undergraduates
Restrictions: Limited to scholarships for men's basketball, men's and women's cross country and soccer, women's volleyball
$ Given: 10 grants for men and women ('92-'93)
Deadline: Contact the department coach
Contact: Mr. Gary Zane, Athletic Director

University of Maine
Orono, ME 04469
(207) 581-1057

Description: Athletic scholarships for undergraduates
Restrictions: Limited to scholarships for men's baseball, men's and women's basketball, women's field hockey, men's football, ice hockey and soccer, women's softball, men's swimming, men's and women's swimming-diving, men's track and field
$ Given: Unspecified number of awards ranging: $100-$12,500 (full tuition)
Deadline: Contact the department coach
Contact: Mr. Michael Ploszek, Athletic Director

. . . .

MARYLAND

Bowie State University
Bowie, MD 20715
(301) 464-6514

Description: Athletic scholarships for undergraduates
Restrictions: Limited to scholarships for men's baseball, men's and women's basketball, men's and women's cross-country running, men's football, women's softball, men's and women's track and field and women's volleyball
$ Given: Grants ranging $500 - $6,500/9,000 (full tuition)
Deadline: Contact the department coaches
Contact: Charles Guilford, Athletics Director

Columbia Union College
7600 Flower Avenue
Takoma Park, MD 20912
(301) 891-4024

Description: Athletic scholarships for undergraduates
Restrictions: Limited to scholarships for men's and women's basketball, men's and women's cross-country running, men's and women's gymnastics, men's soccer, men's and women's tennis, men's and women's track and field and women's volleyball
$ Given: Grants ranging $500 - $9,500 (basketball, full tuition)
Deadline: Contact the department coaches
Contact: Rick Murrey, Athletic Department Director

Coppin State College
2500 West North Avenue
Baltimore, MD 21216
(410) 383-5688

Description: Athletic scholarships for undergraduates
Restrictions: Limited to scholarships for men's baseball, men's basketball, men's and women's cross-country running, women's softball, men's and women's tennis, men's and women's track and field, women's volleyball and men's wrestling
$ Given: 13 available awards for men totalling $66,241; 10 available awards for women totalling $66,241
Deadline: July 1
Contact: Jesse Batten, Athletics Director

FREE MONEY FOR ATHLETIC SCHOLARSHIPS

• • • • • • • • • • • • • • • • • • • •

Johns Hopkins University
126 Garland Hall
3400 North Charles Street
Baltimore, MD 21218
(410) 516-8028

Description: Athletic scholarships for male undergraduates
Restrictions: Limited to scholarships for men's lacrosse
$ Given: 14 awards for men; average grant ranging up to $17,900 (full tuition)
Deadline: Contact the department coaches
Contact: Ellen Frishberg, Director of Financial Aid

Loyola College
4501 North Charles Street
Baltimore, MD 21210
(410) 617-5014

Description: Athletic scholarships for undergraduates
Restrictions: Limited to scholarships for men's and women's basketball, men's and women's golf, men's and women's lacrosse, men's and women's soccer, men's and women's swimming, men's and women's tennis and women's volleyball
$ Given: 16 awards for men totalling $167,050; 10 awards for women totalling $107,950; average grant: $6,000
Deadline: Contact the department coaches
Contact: James Smith, Assistant Director, Department of Athletics

Mount Saint Mary's College
Emmitsburg, MD 21727
(301) 447-6122

Description: Athletic scholarships for undergraduates
Restrictions: Limited to scholarships for men's baseball, men's and women's basketball, men's and women's cross-country running, men's lacrosse, men's and women's soccer, men's and women's tennis and men's and women's track and field
$ Given: 10 awards for men; 15 awards for women; grants ranging $1,000 - $18,000 (full tuition)
Deadline: Contact the department coaches
Contact: Mr. Joseph Paul Zanella, Director of Financial Aid

• •

**University of Maryland -
Baltimore County**
Baltimore, MD 21228
(410) 455-2290

Description: Athletic scholarships for undergraduates
Restrictions: Limited to scholarships for men's baseball, men's and women's basketball, men's and women's cross-country running, men's golf, men's and women's lacrosse, men's and women's soccer, women's softball, men's and women's swimming and diving, men's and women's tennis, men's and women's track and field and women's volleyball
$ Given: 87 awards for men; 75 awards for women; of varying amounts
Deadline: Contact the department coaches
Contact: David Langford, Academic Advisor

**University of Maryland -
College Park**
Department of Athletics
Post Office Box 0295
College Park, MD 20742
(301) 314-7076

Description: Athletic scholarships for undergraduates
Restrictions: Limited to scholarships for men's baseball, men's and women's basketball, men's and women's cross-country running, women's field hockey, men's football, men's golf, women's gymnastics, men's and women's lacrosse, men's and women's soccer, men's and women's swimming and diving, men's and women's tennis, men's and women's track and field, women's volleyball and men's wrestling
$ Given: Average grant ranging from $7,857 (men) and $7,307 (women) up to full tuition and board
Deadline: Contact the department coaches
Contact: Andy Geiger, Athletics Director

**University of Maryland -
Eastern Shore**
Princess Anne, MD 21853
(410) 651-6496

Description: Athletic scholarships for undergraduates
Restrictions: Limited to scholarships for men's baseball, men's and women's basketball and men's tennis
$ Given: Grants ranging $2,000 - $11,000 (full tuition)
Deadline: February 15, contact the department coaches
Contact: Dr. Hallie Gregory, Athletics Program Director

FREE MONEY FOR ATHLETIC SCHOLARSHIPS

· ·

MASSACHUSETTS

American International College
Springfield, MA 01109
(413) 737-7000 Ext. 334

Description: Athletic scholarships for undergraduates
Restrictions: Limited to scholarships for men's baseball, men's and women's basketball, men's football, women's softball and women's volleyball
$ Given: Grants ranging $1,000 - $13,500
Deadline: Contact the department coaches
Contact: Larry O'Donnell, Athletic Director

Assumption College
500 Salisbury Street
Worcester, MA 01615-0005
(508) 752-5615 Ext. 279

Description: Athletic scholarships for undergraduates
Restrictions: Limited to scholarships for men's and women's basketball
$ Given: Full scholarship awards of $16,000 each
Deadline: March 1, contact the department coaches
Contact: Rita Castagna, Athletics Director

Atlantic Union College
PE Department
South Lancaster, MA 01561
(508) 368-2280

Description: Athletic scholarships for undergraduates
Restrictions: Limited to scholarships for men's basketball and women's volleyball
$ Given: Grants ranging $500 - $5,000
Deadline: Contact the department coaches
Contact: Mr. W. A. Deitemeyer, Director of Financial Aid

Bentley College
175 Forest Street
Waltham, MA 02154-4705
(617) 891-2780

Description: Athletic scholarships for undergraduates
Restrictions: Limited to scholarships for men's and women's basketball
$ Given: 3 available awards for men; 2 available awards for women. Grants average $18,000 each (full tuition)
Deadline: Contact the department coaches
Contact: Sandy Thompson, Academic Advisor

Boston College
Chestnut Hill, MA 02167
(617) 552-4527

Description: Athletic scholarships for undergraduates
Restrictions: Limited to scholarships for men's and women's basketball, men's and women's cross-country running, women's field hockey, men's football, men's ice hockey, men's lacrosse, men's and women's soccer, women's softball, women's swimming and diving, women's tennis, men's and women's track and field and women's volleyball
$ Given: 41 available awards for men totalling $760,898; 16 available awards for women totalling $136,640
Deadline: Contact the department coaches
Contact: Ms. Bobbi Carson, Athletics Department

Boston University
285 Babcock Street
Boston, MA 02215
(617) 353-4683

Description: Athletic scholarships for undergraduates
Restrictions: Limited to scholarships for men's baseball, men's and women's basketball, men's and women's crew, women's field hockey, men's football, men's ice hockey, men's soccer, women's softball, men's and women's swimming and diving, men's and women's tennis, men's and women's track and field and men's wrestling
$ Given: 48 available awards; grants range $5,000 - $22,000 (full tuition)
Deadline: Contact the department coaches
Contact: Larry Fudge, Athletics Department

Merrimack College
Turnpike Road
North Andover, MA 01845
(508) 837-5389

Description: Athletic scholarships for undergraduates
Restrictions: Limited to scholarships for men's and women's basketball and men's ice hockey
$ Given: 10 awards for men; 10 awards for women; average range: $11,000 (full room, board and tuition)
Deadline: Contact the department coaches
Contact: Robert DeGregorio, Director of Athletics

• •

**University of
Massachusetts at Amherst**
Amherst, MA 01003
(413) 545-2460

Description: Athletic scholarships for undergraduates
Restrictions: Limited to scholarships for men's baseball, men's and women's basketball, men's and women's cross-country running, women's field hockey, men's football, men's and women's gymnastics, men's and women's lacrosse, women's soccer, women's softball, men's and women's swimming and diving, men's and women's track and field, women's volleyball and men's water polo
$ Given: Grants ranging $500 - $16,000 (full scholarship out-of-state) and $9,000 for in-state resident
Deadline: Contact the department coaches
Contact: Al Rufe, Assistant Director, Athletics Department

**University of
Massachusetts - Lowell**
Lowell, MA 01854
(508) 934-4233

Description: Athletic scholarships for undergraduates
Restrictions: Limited to scholarships for men's and women's basketball, men's and women's cross-country running, women's field hockey, men's ice hockey, men's swimming and diving, men's and women's tennis, men's and women's track and field, women's volleyball and men's wrestling
$ Given: Grants averaging $1,847 (tuition)
Deadline: Contact the department coaches
Contact: Mr. Barrett, Scholarship Coordinator

MICHIGAN

Aquinas College
Grand Rapids, MI 49506-1799
(616) 459-8281, (800) 678-9593

Description: Athletic scholarships for undergraduates
Restrictions: Limited to scholarships for men's baseball, men's and women's basketball, men's and women's cross-country running, men's and women's golf, men's soccer, women's softball, men's and women's tennis, men's and women's track and field and women's volleyball
$ Given: 27 awards for men; 10 awards for women; average range: $200 - $2,000
Deadline: Contact the department coaches
Contact: Mr. Dave Steffee, Director of Financial Aid

. . . .

**Central Michigan
University**
Mount Pleasant, MI 48859
(517) 774-3674

Description: Athletic scholarships for undergraduates
Restrictions: Limited to scholarships for men's baseball, men's and women's basketball, men's and women's cross-country running, women's field hockey, men's football, women's gymnastics, men's soccer, men's and women's track and field, women's volleyball and men's wrestling
$ Given: 37 available awards for men totalling $172,038; 20 available awards for women totalling $73,731; average grant $8,550 (tuition)
Deadline: Contact the department coaches
Contact: Ms. Linda Mrochinski, Assistant Director of Financial Aid

Concordia College
Ann Arbor, MI 48105
(313) 995-7342

Description: Athletic scholarships for undergraduates
Restrictions: Limited to scholarships for men's and women's basketball
$ Given: 6 available awards for men totalling $7,200; 6 available awards for women totalling $7,200; average grant for men $1,000 - $4,000, average grant for women $1,700 - 2,000
Deadline: Contact the department coaches
Contact: Mr. Brian Heinemann, Director of Financial Aid

**Detroit College of
Business**
Dearborn, MI 48126
(313) 581-4400 Ext. 262

Description: Athletic scholarships for male undergraduates
Restrictions: Limited to scholarships for men's golf and men's soccer
$ Given: 12 available awards for men (8 for soccer, 4 for golf) totalling $60,000; average grant $5,000
Deadline: Contact the department coaches
Contact: Kevin Brazell, Athletics Director

FREE MONEY FOR ATHLETIC SCHOLARSHIPS

• •

Detroit College of Business, Warren Campus
27500 Dequindre
Warren, MI 48092
(313) 558-8700

Description: Athletic scholarships for undergraduates
Restrictions: Limited to scholarships for men's golf and men's soccer
$ Given: Grants ranging $500 - $2,160
Deadline: Contact the department coaches
Contact: Ms. Jodi Garner, Athletics Department

Eastern Michigan University
Office of Financial Aid
403 Pierce Hall
Ypsilanti, MI 48197
(313) 487-1050
(Athletic Department)
(313) 487-0455 (Financial Aid)

Description: Athletic scholarships for undergraduates
Restrictions: Limited to scholarships for men's and women's basketball, men's football, men's and women's golf, men's and women's soccer and men's and women's tennis
$ Given: Awards ranging $250 - $8,100 (covering full tuition, room and board)
Deadline: Contact the department coaches
Contact: Mrs. Judy Tatum, Director of Financial Aid

Ferris State University
210 Sports Drive
Big Rapids, MI 49307
(616) 592-2860

Description: Athletic scholarships for undergraduates
Restrictions: Limited to scholarships for men's baseball, men's and women's basketball, men's and women's cross-country running, men's football, women's golf, men's ice hockey, men's and women's swimming and diving, men's and women's tennis, men's and women's track and field, women's volleyball and men's wrestling
$ Given: 78 awards for men; 52 awards for women; average range $500 - $990 (full tuition)
Deadline: Contact the department coaches
Contact: Lisa Wiler, Athletics Department

Grand Valley State University
120 Seidman
Allendale, MI 49401
(616) 895-3234

Description: Athletic scholarships for undergraduates
Restrictions: Limited to scholarships for men's and women's basketball, men's football, women's softball, and women's volleyball
$ Given: Available awards for men and women totalling $300,000; average range $2,600 - $6,800 (full tuition)
Deadline: Contact the department coaches
Contact: Mr. Ken Fridsma, Director of Financial Aid

. . . .

Hillsdale College

Athletic Department
Hillsdale, MI 49242
(517) 437-7341

Description: Athletic scholarships for undergraduates
Restrictions: Limited to scholarships for men's baseball, men's and women's basketball, men's and women's cross-country running, men's football, women's softball, women's swimming and diving, women's tennis, women's track and field and women's volleyball
$ Given: Unspecified number of grants of varying amounts; grants ranging $2,500 - $10,000 (full tuition)
Deadline: Contact the department coaches
Contact: Jack McAvoy, Athletic Director

Lake Superior State University

Athletic Department
1000 College Drive
Sault Sainte Marie, MI
49783
(906) 635-2627

Description: Athletic scholarships for undergraduates
Restrictions: Limited to scholarships for men's and women's basketball, men's and women's cross-country running, men's golf, men's ice hockey, men's and women's tennis, women's volleyball and men's wrestling
$ Given: Numerous awards for men and women ranging $200 up to $7,049 (full scholarship)
Deadline: Contact the department coaches
Contact: Jim Phallis, Athletics Department Director

Michigan Christian College

800 West Avon Road
Rochester Hills, MI 48307
(313) 650-6057

Description: Athletic scholarships for undergraduates
Restrictions: Limited to scholarships for men's and women's basketball, men's and women's cross-country running, men's soccer, men's and women's track and field and women's volleyball
$ Given: 23 awards for men totalling $48,800; 4 awards for women totalling $22,500 (1993); average grant ranges $500 - $3,000
Deadline: Contact the department coaches
Contact: Mr. Garth Pleasant, Director of Athletics

FREE MONEY FOR ATHLETIC SCHOLARSHIPS

• •

Michigan State University
259 Student Services
Building
East Lansing, MI 48824
(517) 353-5940

Description: Athletic scholarships for undergraduates
Restrictions: Limited to scholarships for men's and women's basketball, men's and women's cross-country running, women's field hockey, men's football, men's and women's golf, men's and women's gymnastics, men's ice hockey, men's soccer, men's and women's swimming and diving, men's and women's tennis, men's and women's track and field, women's volleyball and men's wrestling
$ Given: 244 awards for men totalling $1,124,410; 221 awards for women totalling $856,220
Deadline: Contact the department coaches
Contact: Ms. Linda Sigh, Director of Financial Aid

Michigan Technological University
Houghton, MI 49931
(906) 487-2622

Description: Athletic scholarships for undergraduates
Restrictions: Limited to scholarships for men's and women's basketball, men's football, men's ice hockey and women's volleyball
$ Given: 47 awards total for men and women; average range $300 - $11,255 (full tuition, room and board)
Deadline: September 1. Contact the department coaches
Contact: Mr. Timothy T. Malette, Director of Financial Aid; or Rick Yeo, Athletics Director

University of Michigan
Athletics Department
1000 South State
Ann Arbor, MI 48109-2201
(313) 764-1817

Description: Athletic scholarships for undergraduates
Restrictions: Limited to scholarships for men's baseball, men's and women's basketball, men's and women's cross-country running, women's field hockey, men's football, men's and women's golf, women's gymnastics, men's ice hockey, women's softball, men's and women's swimming and diving, men's and women's tennis, men's and women's track and field, women's volleyball and men's wrestling
$ Given: Unspecified number of awards ranging $200 - $22,000 (full scholarship)
Deadline: Contact the department coaches
Contact: Pat Perry, Athletics Department Coordinator

University of Michigan - Dearborn
4901 Evergreen Road
Dearborn, MI 48128
(313) 593-5540

Description: Athletic scholarships for undergraduates
Restrictions: Limited to scholarships for men's and women's basketball and women's volleyball
$ Given: 4 awards for men totalling $4,600; 6 awards for women totalling $6,100; average range $500 - $2,900
Deadline: Contact the department coaches
Contact: Peggy Foss, Athletics Director

MINNESOTA

Bemidji State University
1500 Birchmont Drive NE
Bemidji, MN 56601
(218) 755-2000

Description: Athletic scholarships for undergraduates
Restrictions: Limited to scholarships for men's and women's basketball, men's football, women's tennis, men's and women's track and field and women's volleyball
$ Given: Unspecified number of awards of various amounts ranging up to $2,500
Deadline: Contact the department coaches
Contact: Bob Peters, Director of Athletics

Mankato State University
Mankato, MN 56002-8400
(507) 389-1185

Description: Athletic scholarships for undergraduates
Restrictions: Limited to scholarships for men's baseball, men's and women's basketball, men's and women's cross-country running, men's football, men's and women's golf, men's ice hockey, women's softball, men's and women's swimming and diving, men's and women's tennis, men's and women's track and field, women's volleyball and men's wrestling
$ Given: Unspecified number of awards ranging from $500 - $5,000 (full tuition)
Deadline: Contact Don Amiot, men's coach, or Georgeanne Brock, women's coach
Contact: Jane Watson, Office of Financial Aid

FREE MONEY FOR ATHLETIC SCHOLARSHIPS

• •

Moorhead State University
Athletic Department
Moorhead, MN 56563
(218) 236-2556

Description: Athletic scholarships for undergraduates
Restrictions: Limited to scholarships for men's and women's basketball, men's and women's cross-country running, men's football, men's and women's golf, women's tennis, men's and women's track and field, women's volleyball and men's wrestling
$ Given: 170 awards for men and women; average range $200 - $2,200
Deadline: Contact the department coaches
Contact: Katy Wilson, Athletics Director

University of Minnesota, Duluth
Duluth, MN 55812
(218) 726-8168

Description: Athletic scholarships for undergraduates
Restrictions: Limited to scholarships for men's baseball, men's and women's basketball, men's and women's cross-country running, men's football, men's ice hockey, women's softball, men's and women's tennis, men's and women's track and field, women's volleyball and men's wrestling
$ Given: Various grants ranging from partial to full scholarships ($500 - $6,000)
Deadline: Contact the department coaches
Contact: Bill Haller, Men's Athletic Coordinator

University of Minnesota, Twin Cities Campus
516 15th Avenue SE
Minneapolis, MN 55455
(612) 625-5357

Description: Athletic scholarships for undergraduates
Restrictions: Limited to scholarships for men's and women's basketball, men's and women's cross-country running, men's football, men's and women's golf, men's and women's gymnastics, men's ice hockey, men's and women's swimming and diving, men's and women's tennis, men's and women's track and field, women's volleyball and men's wrestling
$ Given: Unspecified number of awards of various amounts up to full tuition, room and board (approximately $5,816)
Deadline: Contact the department coaches
Contact: Ms. Cheryl Huston, Athletics Director

. . . .

MISSISSIPPI

Alcorn State University
Lorman, MS 39096
(601) 877-6190/6192/6500

Description: Athletic scholarships for undergraduates
Restrictions: Limited to scholarships for men's and women's basketball, men's football, men's and women's tennis and men's and women's track and field
$ Given: Unspecified number of awards; average grant $4,474 (in-state resident) - $6,433 (out-of-state resident)
Deadline: Contact the department coaches
Contact: Ms. Connie Prater, Athletics Coordinator

Belhaven College
1500 Peachtree Street
Jackson, MS 39202-1789
(601) 968-5933/5982

Description: Athletic scholarships for undergraduates
Restrictions: Limited to scholarships for men's baseball, men's and women's basketball, men's and women's cross-country running, men's golf, men's soccer, women's softball, men's and women's tennis and men's and women's track and field
$ Given: Unspecified number of available awards for men and women ranging $2,000 - $9,580 (full scholarship); average range $3,500 - $4,000
Deadline: Contact the department coaches
Contact: Linda Philips, Director of Financial Aid

Blue Mountain College
Athletics Department
Blue Mountain, MS 38610
(601) 685-4771

Description: Athletic scholarships for undergraduates
Restrictions: Limited primarily to scholarships for women's basketball and women's tennis
$ Given: Award averages range $1,500 - $3,718
Deadline: Contact the department coaches
Contact: Ms. Carla Benson, Administrative Assistant to the President

FREE MONEY FOR ATHLETIC SCHOLARSHIPS

Delta State University
Cleveland, MS 38733
(601) 846-4300

Description: Athletic scholarships for undergraduates
Restrictions: Limited to scholarships for men's baseball, men's and women's basketball, women's cross-country running, men's football, men's golf, women's softball, men's and women's swimming and diving, men's and women's tennis and women's track and field
$ Given: Unspecified number of awards for men and women; average ranges $500 - $4,000
Deadline: Contact the department coaches
Contact: Jim Jordan, Director of Athletics

Jackson State University
1325 Lynch Street
Jackson, MS 39217
(601) 968-2291

Description: Athletic scholarships for undergraduates
Restrictions: Limited to scholarships for men's baseball, men's and women's basketball, men's football, men's golf, men's tennis and men's and women's track and field
$ Given: Unspecified number of awards; average range $2,500 - $4,996
Deadline: Contact the department coaches
Contact: Ms. Stephanie Chetman, Acting Director of Financial Aid, or W.C. Gordon, Athletics Department

Mississippi State University
Post Office Box AB
Mississippi State, MS
(601) 325-2533

Description: Athletic scholarships for undergraduates
Restrictions: Limited to scholarships for men's baseball, men's and women's basketball, men's cross-country running, men's football, men's and women's golf, men's and women's tennis, men's track and field and women's volleyball
$ Given: Unspecified number of various awards ranging from partial scholarships to full tuition ($5,703 for in-state residents and $7,600 for out-of-state residents)
Deadline: Contact the department coaches
Contact: Dr. David Boles, Director of Athletics

• •

Mississippi University for Women
Box W-1636
Columbus, MS 39701
(601) 329-7225

Description: Athletic scholarships for undergraduates
Restrictions: Limited to scholarships for women's basketball, women's softball, women's tennis and women's volleyball
$ Given: 33 awards including 10 for basketball, 9 for volleyball, 8 for softball and 6 for tennis; grants ranging $1,500 - $6,400
Deadline: Contact the department coaches
Contact: Michelle Sarrazin, Office of Admissions

University of Mississippi
Athletics Department
25 Old Chemistry Building
University, MS 38677
(601) 232-7122

Description: Athletic scholarships for undergraduates
Restrictions: Limited to scholarships for men's baseball, men's and women's basketball, men's and women's cross-country running, men's football, men's golf, men's and women's tennis, men's and women's track and field and women's volleyball
$ Given: 335 available awards for men and women totalling $1,534,158 and ranging from partial scholarships of $500 to full "head count" scholarships in basketball and football of $3,000 - $4,000
Deadline: Contact the department coaches
Contact: David Wells, Athletics Director

MISSOURI

Avila College
Kansas City, MO 64145
(816) 942-8400 Ext. 223

Description: Athletic scholarships for undergraduates
Restrictions: Limited to scholarships for men's baseball, men's and women's basketball, men's and women's soccer and women's volleyball
$ Given: 21 available awards for men; 21 available awards for women; average grant ranges $1,800 - $10,000
Deadline: Contact the department coaches
Contact: Carl Clapp, Director of Athletics

FREE MONEY FOR ATHLETIC SCHOLARSHIPS

• •

Central Methodist College
Fayette, MO 65248
(816) 248-3391

Description: Athletic scholarships for undergraduates
Restrictions: Limited to scholarships for men's baseball, men's and women's basketball, men's and women's cross-country running, men's football, men's and women's golf, men's and women's soccer, women's softball, men's and women's tennis, men's and women's track and field and women's volleyball
$ Given: Unspecified number of available awards for men and women; general range $500 - $1,500
Deadline: Contact the department coaches
Contact: Larry Anderson, Athletics Department

Central Missouri State University
203 Multipurpose Building
Warrensburg, MO 64093
(816) 543-4250/4290

Description: Athletic scholarships for undergraduates
Restrictions: Limited to scholarships for men's and women's basketball, men's and women's cross-country running, men's football, men's golf, women's softball, men's and women's track and field, women's volleyball and men's wrestling
$ Given: Unspecified number of awards of various amounts ranging $500 - $2,080 (full tuition); average $1,080
Deadline: Contact the department coaches
Contact: Rhonda Crews, Athletics Department

College of the Ozarks
Athletics Department
Point Lookout, MO 65726
(417) 334-6411 Ext. 4290

Description: Athletic scholarships for undergraduates
Restrictions: Limited to scholarships for men's baseball, men's and women's basketball and women's volleyball
$ Given: 12 available awards for each sport; each award totals $1,900 for room and board
Deadline: Contact the department coaches
Contact: Coach Waller, Director

• • • • • • • • • • • • • • • • • • • •

Columbia College
1001 Rogers
Columbia, MO 65216
(314) 875-7410

Description: Athletic scholarships for undergraduates
Restrictions: Limited to scholarships for men's basketball, men's golf, men's soccer, women's softball and women's volleyball
$ Given: Unspecified number of awards for men and women ranging $1,000 - $11,424 (full tuition and board)
Deadline: Contact the department coaches
Contact: Coach Robert Burchard, Athletics Department

Culver-Stockton College
College Hill
Canton, MO 63435
(314) 288-5221 Ext. 306

Description: Athletic scholarships for undergraduates
Restrictions: Limited to scholarships for men's baseball, men's and women's basketball, men's football, men's golf, men's soccer, women's softball, men's and women's tennis and women's volleyball
$ Given: Awards for men and women ranging approximately $500 - $5,000 (one-half tuition, room and board)
Deadline: Contact the department coaches
Contact: Steve Hill, Director of Athletics

Drury College
Springfield, MO 65802
(417) 865-8731

Description: Athletic scholarships for undergraduates
Restrictions: Limited to scholarships for men's basketball, men's golf, men's and women's soccer, men's and women's swimming and diving, men's and women's tennis and women's volleyball
$ Given: Unspecified number of awards for men and women; maximum award of $8,500 (full tuition) for basketball
Deadline: Contact the department coaches
Contact: Dan Cashel, Director of Athletics

Evangel College
Athletic Department
1111 North Glenstone
Springfield, MO 65802
(417) 865-2811/7282

Description: Athletic scholarships for undergraduates
Restrictions: Limited to scholarships for men's and women's basketball, men's and women's cross-country running, men's football, men's and women's track and field and women's volleyball
$ Given: Unspecified number of various partial scholarships up to $6,730 (tuition)
Deadline: Contact the department coaches
Contact: Dr. David Stair, Athletics Director

FREE MONEY FOR ATHLETIC SCHOLARSHIPS

• •

Lincoln University
Athletics Department
212 Jason Gymnasium
Jefferson City, MO 65102-
0029
(314) 681-5326

Description: Athletic scholarships for undergraduates
Restrictions: Limited to scholarships for men's baseball, men's and women's basketball, men's golf, men's soccer, women's softball, women's tennis and men's and women's track and field
$ Given: Unspecified number of awards ranging up to $1,600 (full tuition, in-state resident) - $3,200 (full tuition, out-of-state resident)
Deadline: Contact the department coaches
Contact: Mr. Arnold Woods, Director of Financial Aid

Missouri Southern State College
Athletics Department
3950 East Newman Road
Joplin, MO 64801
(417) 625-9317

Description: Athletic scholarships for undergraduates
Restrictions: Limited to scholarships for men's and women's basketball, men's and women's cross-country running, men's football, men's golf, men's soccer, women's tennis and women's volleyball
$ Given: 27 awards for men and 11 awards for women ranging $2,000 - $5,200 (full tuition, room and board)
Deadline: Contact the department coaches
Contact: Mr. Jim Fraser, Athletics Director

Missouri Western State College
4525 Downs Drive
St. Joseph, MO 64507
(816) 271-4507/4481

Description: Athletic scholarships for undergraduates
Restrictions: Limited to scholarships for men's baseball, men's and women's basketball, men's football, men's golf, women's softball, women's tennis and women's volleyball
$ Given: Unspecified number of various awards ranging $900 - $1,800 (full tuition in-state) and $3,400 (full tuition out-of-state)
Deadline: Contact the department coaches
Contact: Ed Harris, Director of the Athletics Department

· ·

University of Missouri - Columbia
Athletic Department
385 Hearnes
Columbia, MO 65211
(314) 882-5378/2076

Description: Athletic scholarships for undergraduates
Restrictions: Limited to scholarships for men's baseball, men's and women's basketball, men's and women's cross-country running, men's football, men's golf, women's gymnastics, women's softball, men's and women's swimming and diving, men's and women's track and field, women's volleyball and men's wrestling
$ Given: Awards for men and women ranging $200 - $6,433 (full tuition, room and board)
Deadline: Contact the department coaches
Contact: Ms. Kathryn Bass, Assistant Director, Scholarships

University of Missouri - Kansas City
Kansas City, MO 64110
(816) 276-1154

Description: Athletic scholarships for undergraduates
Restrictions: Limited to scholarships for men's and women's basketball, men's and women's cross-country running, men's and women's golf, riflery (m/w), men's soccer, women's softball, men's and women's tennis, and women's volleyball
$ Given: 15 awards for men and 16 awards for women; of various amounts
Deadline: Contact the department coaches
Contact: Dr. Buford Baber, Director of Student Financial Aid

University of Missouri - Rolla
Athletics Department
G-1 Multipurpose Building
Rolla, MO 65401
(314) 341-4175

Description: Athletic scholarships for undergraduates
Restrictions: Limited to scholarships for men's and women's basketball, women's cross-country running, men's football, men's golf, men's and women's soccer, men's swimming and diving and men's track and field
$ Given: 150 awards ranging $2,000 - $3,500 (full tuition in-state) and $7,000 (full tuition out-of-state)
Deadline: Contact the department coaches
Contact: Edith Eaton, Budget and Compliance Officer

• •

University of Missouri - St. Louis
8001 Natural Bridge Road
Normandy, MO 63121-4499
(314) 553-5121

Description: Athletic scholarships for undergraduates
Restrictions: Limited to scholarships for men's baseball, men's and women's basketball, men's golf, men's and women's soccer, women's softball, men's swimming and women's volleyball
$ Given: Unspecified number of various awards ranging up to $2,740 (tuition)
Deadline: Contact the department coaches
Contact: Rich McFessel, Director of Athletics

MONTANA

Carroll College
Athletics Department
Helena, MT 59625
(406) 447-4480

Description: Athletic scholarships for undergraduates
Restrictions: Limited to scholarships for men's and women's basketball, men's football and women's volleyball
$ Given: Unspecified number of available awards for men and women; approximate range $1,000 - $4,000 (partial tuition; full tuition is $7,470)
Deadline: Contact the department coaches
Contact: Rich Wells, Assistant Director of Athletics

Eastern Montana College
1500 North 30th Street
Billings, MT 59101
(406) 657-2369/2603

Description: Athletic scholarships for undergraduates
Restrictions: Limited to scholarships for men's and women's basketball, men's and women's cross-country running, men's and women's tennis and women's volleyball
$ Given: Unspecified number of various awards ranging $1,800 (tuition) - $6,000 (full scholarship, in-state resident) and $8,000 (full scholarship, out-of-state resident)
Deadline: Contact the department coaches
Contact: Gary Nelson, Director of Athletics

• •

Montana College of Mineral Science and Technology
Athletics Department
West Park Street
Butte, MT 59701
(406) 496-4292

Description: Athletic scholarships for undergraduates
Restrictions: Limited to scholarships for men's and women's basketball, men's football and women's volleyball
$ Given: 7 awards for men and 7 awards for women ranging $1,809 (tuition, in-state resident) - $6,055 (full scholarship, out-of-state resident)
Deadline: Contact the department coaches
Contact: Bob Green, Director of Athletics

Montana State University
#135 Strand Union Building
(or Men's Athletics)
Bozeman, MT 59717
(406) 994-2241

Description: Athletic scholarships for undergraduates
Restrictions: Limited to scholarships for men's and women's basketball, men's and women's cross-country running, men's football, men's and women's tennis, men's and women's track and field and women's volleyball
$ Given: Unspecified number of various awards ranging up to $4,000 (full tuition, room and board, in-state resident) - $7,600 (full tuition, room and board, out-of-state resident)
Deadline: Contact the department coaches
Contact: Mr. Dan Davies, Assistant Director of Athletics

University of Montana
Athletics
Missoula, MT 59812
(406) 243-5348

Description: Athletic scholarships for undergraduates
Restrictions: Limited to scholarships for men's and women's basketball, men's and women's cross-country running, men's football, men's and women's tennis, men's and women's track and field and women's volleyball
$ Given: 20 awards for men totalling $100,338; 10 awards for women totalling $40,658
Deadline: Contact the department coaches
Contact: Jane Felsted, Administrative Coordinator

FREE MONEY FOR ATHLETIC SCHOLARSHIPS

• • • • • • • • • • • • • • • • • • • •

NEBRASKA

Bellevue College
1000 Galvin Road South
Bellevue, NB 68005
(402) 293-3781

Description: Athletic scholarships for undergraduates
Restrictions: Limited to scholarships for men's baseball, men's basketball and women's volleyball
$ Given: Unspecified amount of awards; general range $100 - $3,000
Deadline: Contact the department coaches
Contact: Jerry Mosser, Athletics Director

Chadron State College
Athletics Department
1000 Maine
Chadron, NB 69337
(308) 432-6230

Description: Athletic scholarships for undergraduates
Restrictions: Limited to scholarships for men's and women's basketball, men's and women's equestrian sports, men's football, women's golf, men's rodeo, men's and women's track and field, women's volleyball and men's wrestling
$ Given: Unspecified number of awards ranging $200 - $4,091 (full scholarship, in-state resident) and $5,186 (full scholarship, out-of-state resident)
Deadline: Contact the department coaches
Contact: Brad Smith, Director of Athletics

College of Saint Mary
1901 South 72nd Street
Omaha, NB 68124
(402) 399-2451

Description: Athletic scholarships for undergraduates
Restrictions: Limited to scholarships for women's softball, women's tennis and women's volleyball
Restrictions: Primarily for women
$ Given: 9 available awards of various amounts
Deadline: Contact the department coaches
Contact: Ron Romine, Director of Athletics

• • • • • • • • • • • • • • • • • • •

Concordia College
Athletic Department
Seward, NB 68434
(402) 643-7334

Description: Athletic scholarships for undergraduates
Restrictions: Limited to scholarships for men's baseball, men's and women's basketball, men's and women's cross-country running, men's football, men's and women's golf, men's soccer, men's and women's tennis, men's and women's track and field and women's volleyball
$ Given: 40 available awards for men and 25 available awards for women; ranging $200 - $5,000; average $1,500
Deadline: Contact the department coaches
Contact: Courtney Myer, Assistant Director of Athletics

Creighton University
California at 24th Street
Omaha, NB 68178
(402) 280-2731

Description: Athletic scholarships for undergraduates
Restrictions: Limited to scholarships for men's baseball, men's and women's basketball, men's and women's cross-country running, men's and women's golf, men's and women's soccer, women's softball, men's and women's tennis and women's volleyball
$ Given: 25 available awards for men; 14 available awards for women. No totals stated (1993)
Deadline: Contact the department coaches
Contact: Mrs. Mary Johnson, Assistant Director of Financial Aid

Dana College
Pioneer Memorial
2848 College Drive
Blair, NB 68008-9905
(402) 426-7296

Description: Athletic scholarships for undergraduates
Restrictions: Limited to scholarships for men's baseball, men's and women's basketball, men's football, women's softball, women's volleyball and men's wrestling
$ Given: Various number of awards ranging $2,000 - $11,910 (full tuition, room and board); average $3,000
Deadline: Contact the department coaches
Contact: Leo McKillip, Athletics

FREE MONEY FOR ATHLETIC SCHOLARSHIPS

• •

Doane College
Crete, NB 68333
(402) 826-8281

Description: Athletic scholarships for undergraduates
Restrictions: Limited to scholarships for men's baseball, men's and women's basketball, men's and women's cross-country running, men's football, men's and women's golf, women's softball, men's and women's track and field and women's volleyball
$ Given: Available awards for men and women ranging $500 - $3,500
Deadline: Contact the department coaches
Contact: Bob Ericson, Director of Athletics

Midland Lutheran College
900 North Clarkson Street
Fremont, NB 68025
(402) 721-5480

Description: Athletic scholarships for undergraduates
Restrictions: Limited to scholarships for men's and women's basketball, men's and women's cross-country running, men's football, men's and women's golf, men's and women's tennis, men's and women's track and field and women's volleyball
$ Given: Unspecified number of scholarships of various amounts covering partial tuition ($9,550)
Deadline: Contact the department coaches
Contact: Steve Schneider, Director of Athletics

University of Nebraska at Kearney
905 West 25th Street
Kearney, NB 68849
(308) 234-8520

Description: Athletic scholarships for undergraduates
Restrictions: Limited to scholarships for men's and women's basketball, men's and women's cross-country running, men's football, men's and women's golf, women's swimming and diving, men's and women's tennis, men's and women's track and field, women's volleyball and men's wrestling
$ Given: Unspecified number of awards of various amounts
Deadline: Contact the department coaches
Contact: Mr. Pat McTee, Director of Financial Aid

•   •   •   •   •   •   •   •   •   •   •   •   •   •   •   •   •   •   •   •

University of Nebraska at Omaha
EAB
60th and Dodge Streets
Omaha, NB 68182
(402) 554-2305

Description: Athletic scholarships for undergraduates
Restrictions: Limited to scholarships for men's baseball, men's and women's basketball, women's cross-country running, men's football, women's softball, women's volleyball and men's wrestling
$ Given: Awards cover half of tuition cost; partial scholarships ranging $1,000 (in-state resident) - $2,500 (out-of-state resident)
Deadline: Contact the department coaches
Contact: Mike Denny, Director of Athletics

University of Nebraska - Lincoln
Lincoln, NB 68588
(402) 472-2030
(402) 472-3644 (Athletics Department)

Description: Athletic scholarships for undergraduates
Restrictions: Limited to scholarships for men's baseball, men's and women's basketball, men's and women's cross-country running, men's football, men's and women's golf, men's and women's gymnastics, women's softball, men's and women's swimming and diving, men's and women's tennis, men's and women's track and field, women's volleyball and men's wrestling
$ Given: 259 available awards for men totalling $1,254,308; 139 available awards for women totalling $560,595; ranging $200 - $3,700 (full awards for men's basketball, men's football, women's gymnastics and women's volleyball)
Deadline: Contact the department coaches
Contact: Linda Olson, Athletics Coordinator, or Bill Byrne, Athletic Department Director

NEVADA

University of Nevada, Las Vegas
Athletics Department
4505 Maryland Parkway
Las Vegas, NV 89154
(702) 895-4729

Description: Athletic scholarships for undergraduates
Restrictions: Limited to scholarships for men's baseball, men's and women's basketball, women's cross-country running, men's football, men's golf, men's soccer, women's softball, men's and women's swimming and diving, men's and women's tennis and women's track and field
$ Given: Unspecified number of awards for men totalling $239,474 and for women totalling $136,880; ranging $500 - $12,000 (full out-of-state resident tuition, room and board for football, basketball and tennis)
Deadline: Contact the department coaches
Contact: Jim Weaver, Athletics Director

89

• • • • • • • • • • • • • • • • • • •

**University of Nevada,
Reno**
203 TSS
Reno, NV 89557
(702) 784-6900/6955

Description: Athletic scholarships for undergraduates
Restrictions: Limited to scholarships for men's baseball, men's and women's basketball, men's and women's cross-country running, men's football, men's golf, cross-country skiing (m), downhill skiing (m), women's swimming and diving, men's and women's tennis, men's track and field and women's volleyball
$ Given: 262 awards for men and women of various amounts
Deadline: Contact the department coaches
Contact: Suzanne Bach, Athletic Department Director

NEW HAMPSHIRE

Colby-Sawyer College
New London, NH 03257
(603) 526-2010

Description: Gives competitive financial aid packages (work-study grants and loans)
Restrictions: No athletic scholarships given but competitive sports include: men's and women's alpine racing, men's basketball, men's and women's downhill skiing and men's soccer
$ Given: Varying amounts of aid packages are given (work-study and loans, grants, etc.)
Deadline: February 15th
Contact: Ms. Deborah McGrath, Director of Athletics, or John Yatchison, Director of Financial Aid

Franklin Pierce College
College Road
Post Office Box 60
Rindge, NH 03461-0060
(603) 899-4080

Description: Athletic scholarships for undergraduates
Restrictions: Limited to scholarships for men's and women's basketball, men's and women's soccer, women's softball, men's and women's tennis and women's volleyball
$ Given: Unspecified number of awards for men and women ranging $1,000 - $17,270
Deadline: Contact the department coaches
Contact: Bruce Kirsh, Director of Athletics

Keene State College
Athletic Department
229 Main Street
Keene, NH 03431
(603) 358-2813

Description: Athletic scholarships for undergraduates
Restrictions: Limited to scholarships for men's baseball, men's and women's basketball, men's and women's cross-country running, men's and women's soccer, women's softball
$ Given: Need-based awards ranging $200 - $11,000 (full awards for men's and women's basketball and men's and women's soccer)
Deadline: Contact the department coaches
Contact: Joanne Fortunato, Director of Athletics

University of New Hampshire
Stoke Hall
Durham, NH 03824
(603) 862-1850 Ext. 2013

Description: Athletic scholarships for undergraduates
Restrictions: Limited to scholarships for men's and women's basketball, women's field hockey, men's football, women's gymnastics, men's and women's ice hockey, women's lacrosse, men's cross-country skiing, women's downhill skiing, women's soccer, women's swimming and diving and women's track and field
$ Given: 29 awards for men and 12 awards for women of varying amounts
Deadline: Contact the department coaches
Contact: Mr. Gib Chapman, Director of Athletics

NEW JERSEY

Bloomfield College
Bloomfield, NJ 07003
(201) 748-9000 Ext. 212

Description: Athletic scholarships for undergraduates
Restrictions: Limited to scholarships for men's baseball, men's and women's basketball, men's soccer, women's softball and women's volleyball
$ Given: 12 available awards for men; 12 available awards for women; average range: $2,000 - $8,000 (full tuition)
Deadline: April 15th. Contact the department coaches
Contact: Sheila Wooten, Assistant Director of Athletics

FREE MONEY FOR ATHLETIC SCHOLARSHIPS

• • • • • • • • • • • • • • • • • • • •

Caldwell College
Ryerson Avenue
Caldwell, NJ 07006
(201) 228-4424 Ext. 264

Description: Athletic scholarships for undergraduates
Restrictions: Limited to scholarships for men's and women's basketball, men's soccer and women's softball
$ Given: Unspecified number of awards ranging $500 - $5,000
Deadline: Contact the department coaches
Contact: Mark Corino, Athletics Department Director

Georgian Court College
900 Lakewood Avenue
Lakewood, NJ 08701-2697
(908) 363-2374

Description: Athletic scholarships for undergraduates
Restrictions: Limited to scholarships for women's basketball, women's cross-country running, women's soccer and women's softball
$ Given: 15 available awards for women totalling $40,000; partial to full ($8,450) scholarships
Deadline: Contact the department coaches
Contact: Kathy Perri, Athletics Director

Monmouth College
West Long Branch, NJ
07764-1898
(908) 571-3415

Description: Athletic scholarships for undergraduates
Restrictions: Limited to scholarships for men's and women's basketball, men's and women's cross-country running, men's and women's soccer, men's and women's tennis and men's and women's track and field
$ Given: Awards ranging $2,000 - $16,800 (full tuition, basketball)
Deadline: Contact the department coaches
Contact: Joan Martin, Associate Director, Department of Athletics

NEW MEXICO

College of the Southwest
6610 Lovington Highway
Hobbs, NM 88240
(505) 392-6561 Ext. 208

Description: Athletic scholarships for undergraduates
Restrictions: Limited to scholarships for men's baseball and men's and women's soccer
$ Given: Varying amounts of awards ranging $500 - $2,000; average $1,600
Deadline: June 1. Contact the department coach, Jerome Hickey
Contact: Dr. Kashner, Director of Athletics

. . . .

Eastern New Mexico University
Greyhound Arena 17,
Athletics
Portales, NM 88130
(800) 367-3668
(505) 562-1011 Ext. 2153

Description: Athletic scholarships for undergraduates
Restrictions: Limited to scholarships for men's baseball, men's and women's basketball, men's football, men's and women's riflery, women's tennis and women's volleyball
$ Given: Numerous awards for men and women ranging up to $7,000 (in-state resident) and $4,300 (out-of-state resident)
Deadline: Contact the department coaches
Contact: Bibi Lees, Director of Athletics

University of New Mexico
Athletics
Johnson Center
Albuquerque, NM 87131-2039
(505) 277-6536

Description: Athletic scholarships for undergraduates
Restrictions: Limited to scholarships for men's and women's basketball, men's and women's cross-country running, men's football, men's and women's golf, men's gymnastics, men's and women's cross-country skiing, men's and women's downhill skiing, men's soccer, women's softball, men's and women's swimming and diving, men's and women's tennis, men's and women's track and field, women's volleyball and men's wrestling
$ Given: 40 awards for men totalling $220,951; 26 awards for women totalling $167,951 ranging up to $6,080 (full tuition, room and board)
Deadline: Contact the department coaches
Contact: Cheryl Weidener, Academic Advisor

NEW YORK

Adelphi University
Woodruff Hall
Garden City, NY 11530
(516) 877-4240

Description: Athletic scholarships for undergraduates
Restrictions: Limited to scholarships for men's baseball, men's and women's basketball, women's cross-country running, men's lacrosse, men's and women's soccer and men's and women's tennis
$ Given: Unspecified number of awards for men and women; average range: $6,000 - $11,200
Deadline: Contact the department coaches
Contact: Robert Hartwell, Athletics Director

FREE MONEY FOR ATHLETIC SCHOLARSHIPS

• • • • • • • • • • • • • • • • • • •

Canisius College
2001 Main Street
Buffalo, NY 14208
(716) 888-2970

Description: Athletic scholarships for undergraduates
Restrictions: Limited to scholarships for men's baseball, men's and women's basketball, men's and women's cross-country running, men's ice hockey, men's lacrosse, men's and women's riflery, men's and women's soccer, women's softball, men's swimming and diving, men's and women's tennis, men's and women's track and field and women's volleyball
$ Given: Unspecified number of awards of varying amounts ranging from partial scholarships to full (for men's and women's basketball, $9,500)
Deadline: Contact the department coaches
Contact: Dr. Daniel Starr, Department of Athletics Director

Clarkson University
Potsdam, NY 13699
(315) 268-6616
(315) 268-3874

Description: Athletic scholarships for undergraduates
Restrictions: Limited to scholarships for men's ice hockey
$ Given: 23 available awards ranging up to $15,060
Deadline: Contact the department coach, Mark Morris
Contact: William O'Flaherty, Athletic Department Director

College of Saint Rose
Albany, NY 12203
(518) 454-5282

Description: Athletic scholarships for undergraduates
Restrictions: Limited to scholarships for men's and women's basketball, men's and women's cross-country running, women's swimming and diving, women's tennis and women's volleyball
$ Given: 33 available awards for men and women of varying amounts
Deadline: Contact the department coaches
Contact: Kathy Haker, Director of Athletics

- -

Concordia College
Bronxville, NY 10708-1998
(914) 337-9300 Ext. 2450

Description: Athletic scholarships for undergraduates
Restrictions: Limited to scholarships for men's and women's basketball, men's soccer, men's and women's tennis and men's and women's volleyball
$ Given: Unspecified number of awards of varying amounts up to full tuition ($9,990)
Deadline: Contact the department coaches
Contact: Randy Gast, Director of Athletics Department

Daemen College
4380 Main Street
Amherst, NY 14226
(716) 839-3600 Ext. 8346

Description: Athletic scholarships for undergraduates
Restrictions: Limited to scholarships for men's and women's basketball
$ Given: Unspecified number of available awards for men and women; average range: $500 - $8,000 (full tuition)
Deadline: Contact the department coaches
Contact: Donald Delbello, Director of Athletics

Dominican College of Blauvelt
Athletics Department
Western Highway
Orangeburg, NY 10962
(914) 359-6827

Description: Athletic and academic scholarships for undergraduates
Restrictions: Limited to scholarships for men's baseball, men's and women's basketball, men's golf, men's and women's soccer, women's softball and women's volleyball
$ Given: 25 awards for men and 25 awards for women; of varying amounts up to $7,700 (full tuition)
Deadline: Contact the department coaches
Contact: Mr. Joe Clinton, Director of Athletics

Dowling College
Oakdale, NY 11769
(516) 244-3019

Description: Athletic scholarships for undergraduates
Restrictions: Limited to scholarships for men's baseball, men's and women's basketball, men's golf, men's soccer, women's softball, men's and women's tennis and women's volleyball
$ Given: Unspecified number of awards ranging $4,000 - $8,000 (full tuition)
Deadline: Contact the department coaches
Contact: Bob Dranoff, Director of Athletics

FREE MONEY FOR ATHLETIC SCHOLARSHIPS

• •

D'Youville College
320 Porter Avenue
Buffalo, NY 14201
(716) 881-7685

Description: Athletic scholarships for undergraduates
Restrictions: Limited to scholarships for men's and women's basketball and women's volleyball
$ Given: 21 available awards of varying amounts for men and women totalling $13,500
Deadline: Contact the department coaches
Contact: Mr. Murphy, Director of Athletics

Fordham University
Athletic Department
East Fordham Road
Bronx, NY 10458
(212) 579-2447

Description: Athletic scholarships for undergraduates
Restrictions: Limited to scholarships for men's baseball, men's and women's basketball, men's and women's cross-country running, men's football, men's golf, men's soccer, women's softball, men's and women's swimming and diving, men's and women's tennis, men's and women's track and field, women's volleyball and men's water polo
$ Given: Unspecified number of awards of various amounts ranging up to full scholarship (need-based)
Deadline: Contact the department coaches
Contact: Frank McLauglin, Athletics Director

Hofstra University
Athletic Department
Hempstead, NY 11550
(516) 463-6680/6750

Description: Athletic scholarships for undergraduates
Restrictions: Limited to scholarships for men's baseball, men's and women's basketball, women's field hockey, men's and women's lacrosse, men's and women's soccer, women's softball, men's and women's tennis, women's volleyball and men's wrestling
$ Given: Unspecified number of awards for men and women ranging: $1,000 - $11,500 (full scholarships for basketball and volleyball)
Deadline: Contact the department coaches
Contact: Mrs. Kay Pernido, Athletic Coordinator, Office of Financial Aid

• •

Iona College
715 North Avenue
New Rochelle, NY 10801
(914) 633-2304

Description: Athletic scholarships for undergraduates
Restrictions: Limited to scholarships for men's baseball, men's and women's basketball, men's ice hockey, men's and women's soccer, men's and women's swimming, men's tennis, men's track and field and women's volleyball
$ Given: Unspecified number of awards of various amounts ranging: $3,000 - $9,800 (full tuition)
Deadline: Contact the department coaches
Contact: John Norton, Athletics Department

Le Moyne College
Athletics Department
Syracuse, NY 13214
(315) 445-4450

Description: Athletic scholarships for undergraduates
Restrictions: Limited to scholarships for men's baseball, men's and women's basketball, men's and women's cross-country running, men's golf, men's and women's soccer, women's softball, men's and women's tennis and women's volleyball
$ Given: 14 awards for men and 14 awards for women of various amounts ranging up to $10,340 (full tuition)
Deadline: Contact the department coaches
Contact: Dick Rockwell, Director of Athletics

Long Island University, Brooklyn Campus
Athletic Department
One University Plaza
Brooklyn, NY 11201
(718) 488-1030

Description: Athletic scholarships for undergraduates
Restrictions: Limited to scholarships for men's baseball, men's and women's basketball, women's cross-country running, men's golf, men's soccer, women's track and field and women's volleyball
$ Given: Unspecified number of awards for men and women ranging: $5,000 - up to $10,000 (full tuition, room and board)
Deadline: Contact the department coaches
Contact: Paul Lizzo, Director of Athletics

FREE MONEY FOR ATHLETIC SCHOLARSHIPS

. . . .

**Long Island University,
C.W. Post Campus**
Northern Boulevard
Brookville, NY 11548
(516) 299-2288

Description: Athletic scholarships for undergraduates
Restrictions: Limited to scholarships for men's and women's basketball, men's and women's cross-country running, women's field hockey, men's lacrosse, men's soccer, men's and women's track and field and women's volleyball
$ Given: Unspecified number of awards for men and women ranging: $1,000 - $16,000 (full scholarship)
Deadline: Contact the department coaches
Contact: Vincent Salamone, Athletics Director

**Long Island University,
Southampton Campus**
Athletic Department
Southampton, NY 11968
(516) 283-4000 Ext. 386

Description: Athletic scholarships for undergraduates
Restrictions: Limited to scholarships for men's and women's basketball, men's lacrosse, men's and women's soccer, women's softball and men's and women's volleyball
$ Given: 8 awards for men and 8 awards for women ranging: $200 - $10,850 (full tuition)
Deadline: Contact the department coaches
Contact: Mary Topping, Athletic Department Director

Manhattan College
Manhattan College Parkway
Riverdale, NY 10471
(212) 920-0227

Description: Athletic scholarships for undergraduates
Restrictions: Limited to scholarships for men's baseball, men's and women's basketball, men's and women's cross-country running, men's and women's soccer, women's softball, men's and women's tennis, men's and women's track and field, women's volleyball and men's wrestling
$ Given: 67 awards for men and 66 available awards for women; various amounts ranging: $5,000 - full $17,000 for basketball
Deadline: Contact the department coaches
Contact: Mr. Bob Byrnes, Director of Athletics

• •

Marist College
290 North Road
Poughkeepsie, NY 12601-1387
(914) 575-3304 (athletics)

Description: Athletic scholarships for undergraduates
Restrictions: Limited to scholarships for men's baseball, men's and women's basketball, men's and women's diving, men's lacrosse, men's soccer, women's softball, men's and women's swimming, men's and women's tennis, men and women's track and running and women's volleyball
$ Given: Unspecified number of awards ranging: $1,000 - $10,000
Deadline: Contact the department coaches
Contact: Gene Doris, Athletic Director

Mercy College
Athletics Department
555 Broadway
Dobbs Ferry, NY 10522
(914) 674-7220

Description: Athletic scholarships for undergraduates
Restrictions: Limited to scholarships for men's and women's basketball, men's and women's cross-country running, men's and women's golf, men's soccer, men's and women's tennis and women's volleyball
$ Given: Unspecified number of awards for full scholarships covering tuition: $7,000
Deadline: Contact the department coaches
Contact: Neil Judge, Director of Athletics

NORTH CAROLINA

Appalachian State University
Athletics Department
Boone, NC 28608
(704) 262-4010

Description: Athletic scholarships for undergraduates
Restrictions: Limited to scholarships for men's baseball, men's and women's basketball, men's and women's cross-country running, women's field hockey, men's football, men's and women's golf, men's soccer, men's and women's tennis, men's and women's track and field, women's volleyball and men's wrestling
$ Given: Unspecified number of awards of various amounts ranging: $1,000 - $3,700 (in-state residents) and $9,402 (out-of-state residents); basketball, football and volleyball have full awards
Deadline: Contact the department coaches
Contact: Judy Clark, Assistant Director of Athletics

FREE MONEY FOR ATHLETIC SCHOLARSHIPS

• • • • • • • • • • • • • • • • • • • •

Barber-Scotia College
Athletics Department
145 Cabarrus Avenue
Concord, NC 28025
(704) 786-5171

Description: Athletic scholarships for undergraduates
Restrictions: Limited to scholarships for men's and women's basketball, men's softball, men's tennis, women's volleyball and men's wrestling
$ Given: Unspecified number of awards for men and women ranging: $3,000 - $6,600 (full tuition)
Deadline: Contact the department coaches
Contact: Dr. William Madrey, Athletics Director

Barton College
Athletics Department
Post Office Box 5386
West Lee Street
Wilson, NC 27893
(919) 399-6514/6515

Description: Athletic scholarships for undergraduates
Restrictions: Limited to scholarships for men's baseball, men's and women's basketball, men's golf, men's and women's soccer, women's softball, men's and women's tennis and women's volleyball
$ Given: 14 available awards for men and 7 available awards for women; of various amounts ranging from partial scholarships to $10,000
Deadline: Contact the department coaches
Contact: Mr. Gary Hall, Director of Athletics

Belmont Abbey College
Athletics Department
Belmont, NC 28012
(704) 825-6809

Description: Athletic scholarships for undergraduates
Restrictions: Limited to scholarships for men's baseball, men's and women's basketball, women's cross-country, men's golf, men's soccer, men's tennis and women's volleyball
$ Given: Unspecified number of awards ranging: $2,000 - $13,000 (full awards of tuition and room for basketball)
Deadline: Fall. Contact the department coach, Tim Yeager
Contact: Mr. Reidy, Director of Athletics

• •

Campbell University
Athletic Department
Post Office Box 10
Buies Creek, NC 27506
(919) 893-1327 (Athletics)

Description: Athletic scholarships for undergraduates
Restrictions: Limited to scholarships for men's baseball, men's and women's basketball, men's and women's cross-country running, men's and women's golf, men's and women's soccer, women's softball, men's and women's tennis, men's and women's track and field, women's volleyball and men's wrestling
$ Given: 43 available awards for men and 16 available awards for women; of various amounts
Deadline: Contact the department coaches
Contact: Tom Collins, Director of Athletics

Catawba College
2300 West Innes Street
Salisbury, NC 28144-2488
(704) 637-4416
(704) 637-4474 (Athletics)

Description: Athletic scholarships for undergraduates
Restrictions: Limited to scholarships for men's and women's basketball, women's field hockey, men's football, men's golf, men's and women's soccer, women's softball, men's and women's tennis and women's volleyball
$ Given: Approximately 22 available awards for men totalling $66,715 and 25 available awards for women totalling $54,950; all are partial awards, not to exceed $12,950 for tuition, room and board
Deadline: Contact the department coaches
Contact: Ms. Penny M. Rice, Associate Director of Scholarships and Financial Assistance, or Mr. Dennis Haglin, Athletic Department

Chowan College
Murfreesboro, NC 27855
(919) 398-1239
(800) 488-4101 (toll free)

Description: Athletic scholarships for undergraduates
Restrictions: Financial aid is awarded to athletes based on scholastic merit. Limited to scholarships for men's and women's basketball, men's and women's football, men's and women's golf, women's volleyball and men's wrestling
$ Given: Unspecified number of awards ranging up to $10,000 for tuition, room and board
Deadline: Contact the department coaches (Ms. Byrd or Cliff Collins)
Contact: Dr. Scott Colclough, Athletics Director

FREE MONEY FOR ATHLETIC SCHOLARSHIPS

• •

Davidson College
Athletics Department
Post Office Box 1750
Davidson, NC 28036
(704) 892-2373

Description: Athletic scholarships for undergraduates
Restrictions: Limited to scholarships for men's and women's basketball, women's cross-country running, women's field hockey, men's and women's soccer, women's swimming and diving, women's tennis, women's track and field and women's volleyball
$ Given: Unspecified number of awards for men's basketball and soccer and 9 full athletic awards of $20,000
Deadline: Contact the department coaches
Contact: Terry Holland, Athletic Director, or Sterling Martin, Senior Men's Administrator

Duke University
Athletics Department
2138 Campus Drive
Durham, NC 27706
(919) 684-2120

Description: Athletic scholarships for undergraduates
Restrictions: Limited to scholarships for men's baseball, men's and women's basketball, women's field hockey, men's football, men's and women's golf, men's lacrosse, men's and women's soccer, men's and women's tennis, women's volleyball and men's wrestling
$ Given: Large number of awards ranging up to full tuition of $16,720 for men's and women's basketball and men's and women's football
Deadline: Contact the department coaches
Contact: Mr. Tom Butters, Director of Athletics

East Carolina University
Athletics Department
Ward's Building
Greenville, NC 27858-4353
(919) 757-4502

Description: Athletic scholarships for undergraduates
Restrictions: Limited to scholarships for men's baseball, men's and women's basketball, men's and women's cross-country running, men's football, men's golf, men's soccer, women's softball, men's and women's swimming and diving, men's and women's tennis, men's and women's track and field, women's volleyball
$ Given: Unspecified number of awards ranging up to full tuition, room and board for baseball, basketball and football ($4,000 for in-state residents and $7,000 for out-of-state residents)
Deadline: Contact the department coaches
Contact: Mr. Hard, Director of Athletics

· ·

Elon College
Athletics Department
Post Office Box 2500
Elon College, NC 27244
(919) 584-2420

Description: Athletic scholarships for undergraduates
Restrictions: Limited to scholarships for men's baseball, men's and women's basketball, men's and women's cross-country, men's football, men's golf, men's and women's soccer, women's softball, men's and women's tennis, men's track and women's volleyball
$ Given: Unspecified number of awards for men and women ranging $1,150 - $12,290 (full tuition, room and board)
Deadline: Contact the department coaches
Contact: Clay Hassard, Assistant Director of Athletics

Fayetteville State University
Fayetteville, NC 28301
(919) 486-1314 (Athletics)

Description: Athletic scholarships for undergraduates
Restrictions: Limited to scholarships for men's basketball and men's football
$ Given: Unspecified number of awards ranging up to tuition fees of $1,892 (in-state resident) and $4,728 (out-of-state resident)
Deadline: Contact the department coaches
Contact: Dr. Rathburns, Director of Athletics

Lees-McRae College
Post Office Box 128
Banner Elk, NC 28604
(704) 898-5241

Description: Athletic scholarships for undergraduates
Restrictions: Limited to scholarships for men's and women's basketball, men's football, men's downhill skiing, men's and women's soccer and men's and women's tennis
$ Given: 47 available awards for men totalling $95,916 and 19 available awards for women totalling $29,354; partial awards of various amounts
Deadline: Contact the department coaches
Contact: Don Arbaker, Director of Athletics Department

FREE MONEY FOR ATHLETIC SCHOLARSHIPS

• •

Lenoir-Rhyne College
Athletics Department
Box 7227
Hickory, NC 28603
(704) 328-7115

Description: Athletic scholarships for undergraduates
Restrictions: Limited to scholarships for men's baseball, men's and women's basketball, men's and women's cross-country running, men's football, men's golf, men's and women's soccer, women's softball, men's track and field and women's volleyball
$ Given: 48 awards for men totalling $571,680 and 13 awards for women totalling $154,830; of various amounts ranging up to full tuition of $14,060
Deadline: Contact the department coaches
Contact: Ms. Pat Holden, Administrator of the Athletics Department

Livingstone College
Athletics Department
701 West Monroe
Salisbury, NC 28144
(704) 638-5561
(Financial Aid)
(704) 638-5660 (Athletics)

Description: Athletic scholarships for undergraduates
Restrictions: Limited to scholarships for men's and women's basketball, men's football, men's and women's tennis and men's and women's track and field
$ Given: Awards for men totalling $93,855 and awards for women totalling $8,206; partial awards not to exceed tuition and/or room and board ($8,600)
Deadline: Contact the department coaches
Contact: Mr. Tucker, Director of Athletics

Montreat-Anderson College
Montreat, NC 28757
(704) 669-8011 (Financial Aid)
(704) 669-2696 (Athletics)

Description: Athletic scholarships for undergraduates
Restrictions: Limited to scholarships for men's baseball, men's and women's basketball, men's soccer and women's volleyball
$ Given: 19 awards for men and 9 awards for women; average award: $5,000
Deadline: Contact the department coaches
Contact: Steve McNamara, Director of Athletics

University of North Carolina at Asheville
One University Heights
Asheville, NC 28804-3299
(704) 251-6459 (Athletics)

Description: Athletic scholarships for undergraduates
Restrictions: Limited to scholarships for men's baseball, men's and women's basketball, men's and women's cross-country running, men's golf, men's soccer, women's softball, men's and women's tennis, women's track and field and women's volleyball
$ Given: 51 awards for men totalling $118,295 and 37 awards for women totalling $75,559; of various amounts up to $3,000 (tuition, room and board for in-state residents)
Deadline: Contact the department coaches
Contact: Mrs. V. Carolyn McElrath, Director of Financial Aid, or Tom Hunnicutt, Director of Athletics

University of North Carolina at Chapel Hill
Post Office Box 1080
Chapel Hill, NC 27599
(919) 962-2193
(Financial Aid)
(919) 962-6000 (Athletics)

Description: Athletic scholarships for undergraduates
Restrictions: Limited to scholarships for men's and women's basketball, men's and women's cross-country running, men's and women's fencing, women's field hockey, men's football, men's and women's golf, women's gymnastics, men's lacrosse, men's and women's soccer, men's and women's swimming and diving, men's and women's tennis, men's and women's track and field, women's volleyball and men's wrestling
$ Given: Unspecified number of awards ranging up to $3,082 (full tuition, room and board)
Deadline: Contact the department coaches
Contact: Dick Baddour, Associate Director, Athletics Department

University of North Carolina at Charlotte
Charlotte, NC 28223
(704) 547-2461

Description: Athletic scholarships for undergraduates
Restrictions: Limited to scholarships for men's baseball, men's and women's basketball, men's and women's cross-country running, men's golf, men's soccer, women's softball, men's and women's swimming and diving, men's and women's tennis and women's volleyball
$ Given: Unspecified
Deadline: Contact the department coaches
Contact: Mr. Curtis R. Whalen, Director of Financial Aid

• •

University of North Carolina at Greensboro
Athletics Department
Room 337
Health & Human Performance Building
1000 Spring Garden Street
Greensboro, NC 27412-5001
(919) 334-5702
(Financial Aid)
(919) 334-5213
(Athletics Department)

Description: Athletic scholarships for undergraduates
Restrictions: Limited to scholarships for men's baseball, men's and women's basketball, men's and women's cross-country running, men's and women's golf, men's and women's soccer, women's softball, men's and women's tennis, women's volleyball and men's wrestling
$ Given: 21 awards for men totalling $49,962 and 18 awards for women totalling $50,223; ranging up to full awards in basketball and volleyball ($2,800 for men and $2,600 for women)
Deadline: Contact the department coaches
Contact: Nelson Bobb, Director of Athletics

University of North Carolina at Wilmington
Wilmington, NC 28403
(919) 395-3177

Description: Athletic scholarships for undergraduates
Restrictions: Limited to scholarships for men's baseball, men's and women's basketball, men's and women's cross-country running, men's and women's golf, men's soccer, women's softball, men's and women's swimming and diving, men's and women's tennis, men's and women's track and field and women's volleyball
$ Given: Unspecified number of awards
Deadline: Contact the department coaches
Contact: Mr. Joseph V. Capell, Director of Financial Aid

NORTH DAKOTA

Dickinson State University
291 Campus Drive
Dickinson, ND 58601-4896
(701) 227-2181

Description: Athletic scholarships for undergraduates
Restrictions: Limited to scholarships for men's and women's basketball, men's and women's cross-country running, men's football, men's and women's track and field, women's volleyball and men's wrestling
$ Given: Unspecified number of awards for men and women ranging $300 - $400
Deadline: Contact the department coaches
Contact: Mr. Don Lemnus, Director of Athletics

• • • • • • • • • • • • • • • • • • • •

Mayville State University
330 3rd Street NE
Mayville, ND 58257-1299
(701) 786-4869

Description: Athletic scholarships for undergraduates
Restrictions: Limited to scholarships for men's and women's basketball, men's football, women's volleyball and men's wrestling
$ Given: Unspecified number of awards for men and women totalling $11,132; average grant not to exceed $1,800
Deadline: Contact the department coaches
Contact: Mr. David Knoles, Director of Athletics

Minot State University
500 University Avenue West
Minot, ND 58707
(701) 857-3042

Description: Athletic scholarships for undergraduates
Restrictions: Limited to scholarships for men's and women's basketball, men's and women's cross-country running, men's football, men's and women's track and field and women's volleyball
$ Given: 100 awards for men and women; average award not to exceed $1,800 (tuition)
Deadline: Contact the department coaches
Contact: Mr. Fran Hummel, Director of Athletics

University of North Dakota
Athletics Department
Post Office Box 9013
Grand Forks, ND 58202
(701) 777-2234

Description: Athletic scholarships for undergraduates
Restrictions: Limited to awards for men's baseball, men's and women's basketball, men's football, men's ice hockey, women's softball, women's swimming and diving, men's and women's track and field, women's volleyball and men's wrestling
$ Given: Unspecified number of awards; partial and full scholarships ranging: $1,082 - $4,741 (tuition, room and board)
Deadline: Contact the department coaches
Contact: Terry Wanlett, Athletics Department Director, or Pete Oliszczak, Associate Director of Athletics

FREE MONEY FOR ATHLETIC SCHOLARSHIPS

OHIO

Ashland University
Ashland, OH 44805
(419) 289-4142 Ext. 5441

Description: Athletic scholarships for undergraduates
Restrictions: Limited to scholarships for men's baseball, men's and women's basketball, men's and women's cross-country running, men's football, men's golf, women's softball, men's and women's swimming and diving, men's and women's track and field, women's volleyball and men's wrestling
$ Given: 80 awards of varying amounts; full tuition and board of $15,200 for men's basketball
Deadline: Contact the department coaches
Contact: Sue Martinson, Associate Athletic Director

Bowling Green State University
Bowling Green, OH 43403
(419) 372-2651
(419) 372-2401 (Athletics)

Description: Athletic scholarships for undergraduates
Restrictions: Limited to scholarships for men's baseball, men's and women's basketball, men's and women's cross-country running, men's football, men's and women's golf, women's gymnastics, women's softball, men's and women's swimming and diving, men's and women's track and field and women's volleyball
$ Given: Approximately 54 available awards for men and 21 available awards for women; of various amounts ranging up to full tuition, room and board for men's and women's basketball and men's football
Deadline: Contact the department coaches
Contact: Gerry Hutton, Financial Aid Office, or Jack Gregory, Athletics Director

Cedarville College
Athletic Department
P.O. Box 601
Cedarville, OH 45314
(513) 766-2211 Ext. 7755

Description: Athletic scholarships for undergraduates
Restrictions: Limited to scholarships for men's baseball, men's and women's basketball, men's and women's cross-country running, men's golf, men's soccer, women's softball, men's and women's tennis, men's and women's track and field and women's volleyball
$ Given: 5 available awards for men and 10 available awards for women; averaging: $500
Deadline: Contact the department coaches
Contact: Dr. Don Callan, Athletics Department Director

Central State University

Athletics Department
Wilberforce, OH 45384
(513) 376-6289

Description: Athletic scholarships for undergraduates
Restrictions: Limited to scholarships for men's baseball, men's and women's basketball, men's football, men's and women's track and field and women's volleyball
$ Given: Unspecified number of awards; of various amounts ranging up to $6,600 (full tuition for in-state residents) and $9,900 (full tuition for out-of-state residents)
Deadline: Contact the department coaches
Contact: Ms. Sunny Terrell, Director of Student Financial Aid

Cleveland State University

Athletics Department
2000 Prospect Avenue
Cleveland, OH 44115
(216) 687-2000

Description: Athletic scholarships for undergraduates
Restrictions: Limited to scholarships for men's and women's basketball, women's cross-country running, fencing (m/w), men's golf, men's soccer, men's and women's swimming and diving, women's tennis, women's volleyball and men's wrestling
$ Given: 155 available awards for men totalling $480,035 and 70 available awards for women totalling $250,000; ranging up to $992 (full tuition, room, board and books)
Deadline: Contact the department coaches
Contact: John Constantino, Director of Athletics

Kent State University

Athletics Department
Post Office Box 5190
103 Student Services
Center
Kent, OH 44242-0001
(216) 672-2972
(Financial Aid)
(216) 672-3120 (Athletics)

Description: Athletic scholarships for undergraduates
Restrictions: Limited to scholarships for men's and women's basketball, men's and women's cross-country running, women's field hockey, men's football, men's golf, men's and women's gymnastics, men's ice hockey, women's volleyball and men's wrestling
$ Given: Unspecified number of awards ranging: $1,500 - full scholarships in basketball and football of $8,600 (in-state residents) and $12,200 (out-of-state residents)
Deadline: Contact the department coaches
Contact: Mr. William Farthing, Financial Aid Officer, or Paul Amodio, Athletics Director

FREE MONEY FOR ATHLETIC SCHOLARSHIPS

Malone College
Athletics Department
515 25th Street NW
Canton, OH 44709
(216) 471-8300

Description: Athletic scholarships for undergraduates
Restrictions: Limited to scholarships for men's baseball, men's and women's basketball, men's and women's cross-country running, men's football, men's golf, men's soccer, women's softball, men's and women's tennis, men's and women's track and field and women's volleyball
$ Given: 17 awards for men and 16 available awards for women; most awards are partial ($500 - $4,000) but a few full scholarships of $12,500 are given
Deadline: Contact the department coaches
Contact: Hal Smith, Director of Athletics

Miami University
Athletics Department
Millett Hall
Oxford, OH 45056
(513) 529-5757

Description: Athletic scholarships for undergraduates
Restrictions: Limited to scholarships for men's and women's basketball, men's and women's cross-country running, women's field hockey, men's football, men's golf, men's ice hockey, men's and women's swimming and diving, men's and women's tennis, men's and women's track and field, women's volleyball and men's wrestling
$ Given: 60 awards for men totalling $339,486 and 27 awards for women totalling $142,875; awards ranging $200 for books - full scholarships of $8,000 for men's and women's basketball, men's football and women's volleyball
Deadline: Contact the department coaches
Contact: Mr. Johnson, Athletic Director

OKLAHOMA

Bartlesville Wesleyan College
Athletics Department
Bartlesville, OK 74006-6299
(918) 335-6259

Description: Athletic scholarships for undergraduates
Restrictions: Limited to scholarships for men's and women's basketball, men's and women's cross-country running, men's golf, men's and women's soccer, men's tennis and women's volleyball
$ Given: 8 available awards for men and 3 available awards for women; of various amounts ranging up to partial scholarships of $500
Deadline: Contact the department coaches
Contact: Rocky Kent, Athletics Director

• • • • • • • • • • • • • • • • • • • •

East Central University
Athletics Department
Ada, OK 74820
(405) 332-8000 Ext. 314

Description: Athletic scholarships for undergraduates
Restrictions: Limited to scholarships for men's and women's basketball, men's football and men's and women's tennis
$ Given: Unspecified number of awards ranging up to full tuition of $4,000
Deadline: Contact the department coaches
Contact: Dr. Green, Director of Athletics

University of Oklahoma
Athletics Department
731 Elm
Norman, OK 73019-0230
(405) 325-4521

Description: Athletic scholarships for undergraduates
Restrictions: Limited to scholarships for men's baseball, men's and women's basketball, men's and women's cross-country running, men's football, men's and women's golf, men's and women's gymnastics, women's softball, men's and women's tennis, men's and women's track and field, women's volleyball and men's wrestling
$ Given: 17 awards for men totalling $83,787 and 49 available awards for women totalling $237,498; of various amounts
Deadline: Contact the department coaches
Contact: Ms. Mary Mowdy, Interim Director of Financial Aid

OREGON

Concordia College
2811 Northeast Holman
Portland, OR 97211
(503) 280-8514

Description: Athletic scholarships for undergraduates
Restrictions: Limited to scholarships for men's baseball, men's and women's basketball, men's soccer and women's volleyball
$ Given: 30 available awards for men and women ranging: $100 - $9,300 (full tuition)
Deadline: Contact the department coaches
Contact: Mr. Joel Schuldheisz, Director of Athletics

. . . .

University of Oregon
Athletics Department
Eugene, OR 97403
(503) 346-4481

Description: Athletic scholarships for undergraduates
Restrictions: Limited to scholarships for men's and women's basketball, men's and women's cross-country running, men's football, men's golf, women's softball, men's tennis, men's and women's track and field and men's wrestling
$ Given: Unspecified number of awards for partial to full scholarships: $2,000 - $6,000 (in-state residents) and $2,000 - $12,000 (out-of-state residents). Full scholarships given in football.
Deadline: Contact the department coaches
Contact: Mr. Rich Brooks, Director of Athletics Department

University of Portland
Athletics Department
Portland, OR 97203
(503) 283-7117

Description: Athletic scholarships for undergraduates
Restrictions: Limited to scholarships for men's baseball, men's and women's basketball, men's and women's cross-country running, men's golf, men's and women's soccer, men's and women's tennis, men's and women's track and field and women's volleyball
$ Given: 36 awards for men and women totalling $241,407; of various amounts ranging up to $14,000 (full tuition, room and board)
Deadline: Contact the department coaches
Contact: Mr. Joe Ethzel, Director of Athletics

PENNSYLVANIA

Bloomsburg University of Pennsylvania
Ben Franklin Building, Room 19
Bloomsburg, PA 17815
(717) 389-4495 Ext. 4354
(Athletics)

Description: Athletic scholarships for undergraduates
Restrictions: Limited to scholarships for men's baseball, men's and women's basketball, women's field hockey, men's football, women's softball, men's and women's swimming and diving, men's and women's tennis and men's wrestling
$ Given: Unspecified number of awards ranging up to $8,000 (full award)
Deadline: Contact the department coaches
Contact: Mary Gardner, Director of Athletics

• •

California University of Pennsylvania
Athletics Department
California, PA 15419-1394
(412) 938-4351

Description: Athletic scholarships for undergraduates
Restrictions: Limited to scholarships for men's and women's basketball, men's and women's cross-country running, men's football, men's soccer, women's tennis, men's and women's track and field, women's volleyball and men's wrestling
$ Given: Unspecified number of awards of various amounts ranging up to $6,800 (full award). Emphasis on men's and women's basketball, men's football and men's wrestling
Deadline: Contact the department coaches
Contact: Paul Flores, Associate Director of Athletics

Cheyney University of Pennsylvania
Athletics Department
Post Office Box 350
Cheyney, PA 19319
(215) 399-2287

Description: Athletic scholarships for undergraduates
Restrictions: Limited to scholarships for men's and women's basketball, men's and women's cross-country running, men's football, men's and women's tennis, men's and women's track and field, women's volleyball and men's wrestling
$ Given: Unspecified number of awards of various amounts not to exceed $6,500 (full award)
Deadline: Contact the department coaches
Contact: Coach Henson, Athletics Department Director

Clarion University of Pennsylvania
Athletics Department
c/o Tippin Gym
Clarion, PA 16214
(814) 226-1997

Description: Athletic scholarships for undergraduates
Restrictions: Limited to scholarships for men's and women's basketball, men's football, men's golf, women's softball, men's and women's swimming and diving, women's tennis, women's volleyball, and men's wrestling
$ Given: Unspecified number of available awards for men and women ranging $500 - $4,000 in most cases. Full tuition, room and board of $6,500 for basketball and wrestling
Deadline: Contact the department coaches
Contact: Bob Carlson, Director of Athletics

FREE MONEY FOR ATHLETIC SCHOLARSHIPS

• •

Drexel University
Philadelphia, PA 19104
(215) 895-1843

Description: Athletic scholarships for undergraduates
Restrictions: Limited to scholarships for men's baseball, men's basketball, crew (m), men's cross-country running, women's field hockey, men's golf, men's lacrosse, men's soccer, women's softball, men's and women's swimming and diving, men's tennis, men's track and field and men's wrestling
$ Given: 27 available awards for men totalling $198,900 and 19 available awards for women totalling $132,906; of various amounts
Deadline: Contact the department coaches
Contact: Dr. John Gregory, Chief Information Officer, Chief Information Officer

Duquensne University
Athletics Department
Pittsburgh, PA 15282-0299
(412) 434-6607
(412) 434-6565 (Athletics)

Description: Athletic scholarships for undergraduates
Restrictions: Limited to scholarships for men's baseball, men's and women's basketball, men's and women's cross-country running, men's golf, men's and women's riflery, men's and women's swimming and diving, men's and women's tennis, women's track and field, women's volleyball and men's wrestling
$ Given: Unspecified number of available awards for men and women totalling $403,491; ranging from partial awards up to tuition of $16,730 for men's and women's basketball
Deadline: Contact the department coaches
Contact: Brian Colleary, Athletic Director

East Stroudsburg University of Pennsylvania
East Stroudsburg, PA 18301
(717) 424-3340
(Financial Aid)
(717) 424-3642 (Athletics)

Description: Athletic scholarships for undergraduates
Restrictions: Limited to scholarships for men's and women's basketball, men's cross-country running, men's football, men's soccer, men's track and field and men's wrestling
$ Given: 26 available awards for men and 3 available awards for women; of various amounts ranging up to $3,664 (tuition and fees)
Deadline: Contact the department coaches
Contact: Earl Edwards, Athletic Director

Edinboro University of Pennsylvania
Edinboro, PA 16444
(814) 732-2778

Description: Athletic scholarships for undergraduates
Restrictions: Limited to scholarships for men's and women's basketball, men's and women's cross-country running, men's football, men's golf, women's softball, men's and women's swimming and diving, men's and women's tennis, men's and women's track and field, women's volleyball and men's wrestling
$ Given: Unspecified number of awards of various amounts ranging up to $6,552 (full tuition, room and board)
Deadline: Contact the department coaches
Contact: Jim McDonald, Director of Athletics

Gannon University
Athletic Department
University Square
Erie, PA 16541
(814) 871-7337
(814) 871-7416 (Athletics)

Description: Athletic scholarships for undergraduates
Restrictions: Limited to scholarships for men's baseball, men's and women's basketball, men's and women's cross-country running, men's golf, men's and women's soccer, women's softball, men's and women's swimming and diving, men's and women's tennis, women's volleyball and men's wrestling
$ Given: 102 available awards for men totalling $342,200 and 65 available awards for women totalling $218,100; all awards are partial, not to exceed $9,600 (tuition)
Deadline: Contact the department coaches
Contact: Howard Elwell, Director of Athletics

Indiana University of Pennsylvania
308 Pratt Hall
Indiana, PA 15705
(412) 357-2218
(Financial Aid)
(412) 357-2132 (Athletics)

Description: Athletic scholarships for undergraduates
Restrictions: Limited to scholarships for men's and women's basketball, men's and women's cross-country running, men's football and women's gymnastics
$ Given: 27 awards for men and women totalling $39,956 and ranging $2,912 (tuition) - $6,474 (full award)
Deadline: Contact the department coaches
Contact: Mrs. Sally C. Abrams, Associate Director of Financial Aid, or Frank Cignetti, Athletics Director

FREE MONEY FOR ATHLETIC SCHOLARSHIPS

• • • • • • • • • • • • • • • • • • • •

Kutztown University of Pennsylvania
Kutztown, PA 19530
(215) 683-4077
(215) 683-4094 (Athletics)

Description: Athletic scholarships for undergraduates
Restrictions: Limited to scholarships for men's and women's basketball, men's football, men's and women's swimming and diving, men's and women's track and field and men's wrestling
$ Given: Unspecified number of awards ranging up to $3,000 (full tuition, room and board)
Deadline: Contact the department coaches
Contact: Clark Yeager, Director of Athletics

La Salle University
Athletics Department
Hayman Hall
900 West Olney
Box 805
Philadelphia, PA 19141
(215) 951-1070
(Financial Aid)
(215) 951-1516 (Athletics)

Description: Athletic scholarships for undergraduates
Restrictions: Limited to scholarships for men's baseball, men's and women's basketball, men's and women's cross-country running, women's field hockey, men's and women's golf, men's and women's soccer, women's softball, men's and women's swimming and diving, men's and women's tennis, men's and women's track and field and women's volleyball
$ Given: Unspecified number of available awards for men totalling $98,048 and for women totalling $127,559; of various amounts ranging up to full awards of $17,260 (tuition, room and board)
Deadline: Contact the department coaches
Contact: Bob Mullen, Director of Athletics

Lock Haven University of Pennsylvania
Thomas Field House
Lock Haven, PA 17745
(717) 893-2344
(717) 893-2102 (Athletics Department)

Description: Athletic scholarships for undergraduates
Restrictions: Limited to scholarships for men's baseball, men's and women's basketball, women's field hockey, men's football, men's soccer, women's softball, men's and women's track and field, women's volleyball and men's wrestling
$ Given: 15 awards for men and 8 awards for women; ranging $300 for books - $3,800 (wrestling only)
Deadline: Contact the department coaches
Contact: Sharon Taylor, Director of Athletics

Mansfield University of Pennsylvania
107 South Hall
Mansfield, PA 16933
(717) 662-4129

Description: Athletic scholarships for undergraduates
Restrictions: Limited to scholarships for men's and women's basketball and men's football
$ Given: Unspecified number of awards of various amounts
Deadline: Contact the department coaches
Contact: Mr. Christopher W. Vaughn, Director of Financial Aid

Mercyhurst College
Athletics Department
Erie, PA 16546
(814) 824-2240
(Financial Aid)
(814) 824-2558 (Athletics)

Description: Athletic scholarships for undergraduates
Restrictions: Limited to scholarships for men's baseball, men's and women's basketball, men's and women's crew, men's and women's cross-country running, men's and women's golf, men's ice hockey, men's and women's soccer, women's softball, men's and women's tennis and women's volleyball
$ Given: 28 awards for men totalling $92,405 and 35 awards for women totalling $63,136; ranging up to full tuition ($9,200)
Deadline: Contact the department coaches
Contact: Pete Russo, Director of Athletics

Millersville University of Pennsylvania
Athletics Department
Post Office Box 1002
Millersville, PA 17551-0302
(717) 872-3026
(Financial Aid)
(717) 872-3361
(Men's Athletics)

Description: Athletic scholarships for undergraduates
Restrictions: Limited to scholarships for men's baseball, men's and women's basketball, men's and women's cross-country running, women's field hockey, men's football, men's golf, women's lacrosse, men's soccer, women's softball, women's swimming and diving, men's and women's tennis, men's and women's track and field and men's wrestling
$ Given: 35 partial awards for men and women; of various amounts not to exceed $2,828 (tuition) - $3,620 (tuition, room and board)
Deadline: Contact the department coaches
Contact: Mr. Gene R. Wise, Director of Financial Aid, or Dr. Gene Carpenter, Director of Athletics

• •

University of Pittsburgh
Bruce Hall, Second Floor
Pittsburgh, PA 15260
(412) 624-7488
(Financial Aid)
(412) 648-8230 (Athletics)

Description: Athletic scholarships for undergraduates
Restrictions: Limited to scholarships for men's baseball, men's and women's basketball, men's and women's cross-country running, men's football, men's and women's gymnastics, men's soccer, men's and women's swimming and diving, men's and women's tennis, men's and women's track and field, women's volleyball and men's wrestling
$ Given: 59 awards for men and women totalling $288,200; of various amounts
Deadline: Contact the department coaches
Contact: Oval Jaynes, Director of Athletics, or Donna Sanft, Associate Director

RHODE ISLAND

Bryant College
Athletics Department
1150 Douglas Pike
Smithfield, RI 02917-1284
(401) 232-6020
(401) 232-6070 (Athletics)

Description: Athletic scholarships for undergraduates
Restrictions: Limited to scholarships for men's and women's basketball
$ Given: 3 available awards for men and 2 available awards for women ranging up to full grants of $17,000
Deadline: Contact the department coaches, Ed Reilly or Mary Burke
Contact: Linda Hackett, Director of Athletics

University of Rhode Island
Kingston, RI 02881
(401) 792-2314
(Financial Aid)
(401) 792-5245 (Athletics)

Description: Athletic scholarships for undergraduates
Restrictions: Limited to scholarships for men's baseball, men's and women's basketball, men's and women's cross-country running, women's field hockey, men's football, women's gymnastics, men's and women's soccer, women's softball, men's and women's swimming and diving, men's and women's track and field and women's volleyball
$ Given: Unspecified number of awards for men and women ranging up to $7,200 (full tuition, room and board)
Deadline: Contact the department coaches
Contact: Ron Petro, Director of Athletics

• •

SOUTH CAROLINA

**Charleston Southern
University**
Post Office Box 10087
Charleston, SC 29411
(803) 863-8034
(803) 863-7675 (Athletics
Department)

Description: Athletic scholarships for undergraduates
Restrictions: Limited to scholarships for men's baseball,
men's and women's basketball, men's and women's
cross-country running, men's and women's golf, men's
and women's soccer, women's softball, men's and
women's tennis, men's and women's track and field and
women's volleyball
$ Given: 8 available awards for men and 8 available
awards ranging up to full scholarship ($10,200 on
campus)
Deadline: Contact the department coaches
Contact: Howard Bagwell, Athletics Director

**The Citadel, The Military
College of South Carolina**
Charleston, SC 29409
(803) 792-5187
(803) 792-5030 (Athletic
Department)

Description: Athletic scholarships for undergraduates
Restrictions: Limited to scholarships for men's baseball,
men's basketball, men's cross-country running, men's
football, men's golf, men's soccer, men's tennis, men's
track and field and men's wrestling
$ Given: 200 available awards for men totalling $900,000;
70 full scholarships for football
Deadline: Contact the department coaches
Contact: Major Hank M. Fuller, Director of Financial Aid
and Scholarships

Claflin College
700 College Avenue
Orangeburg, SC 29115
(803) 534-2710 Ext. 344
(803) 535-5362
(Athletic Department)

Description: Athletic scholarships for undergraduates
Restrictions: Limited to scholarships for men's and
women's basketball, men's and women's tennis and
men's and women's track
$ Given: 12 awards for men totalling $30,000; 12 awards
for women totalling $30,000; partial scholarships ranging
up to $7,000 per year (tuition)
Deadline: Contact the department coaches (Coach
Brownlee)
Contact: Ms. Yvonne C. Clarkson, Director of Student
Financial Aid, or Dr. Stiff, Athletics Department

FREE MONEY FOR ATHLETIC SCHOLARSHIPS

Clemson University
G01 Sikes Hall
Clemson, SC 29634-5123
(803) 656-2101

Description: Athletic scholarships for undergraduates
Restrictions: Limited to scholarships for men's and women's basketball, men's and women's cross-country running, men's football, men's golf, women's soccer (1994), men's and women's swimming and diving, men's and women's tennis, men's and women's track and field, women's volleyball and men's wrestling
$ Given: Unspecified number of available awards for men and women ranging: $200 (books) up to full scholarships of $12,800 per year for basketball and football
Deadline: Contact the department coaches
Contact: Ms. Shirley Brown, Scholarship Coordinator

College of Charleston
66 George Street
Charleston, SC 29424-0001
(803) 792-5540
(803) 792-5556 (Athletic Department)

Description: Athletic scholarships for undergraduates
Restrictions: Limited to scholarships for men's baseball, men's and women's basketball, men's and women's cross-country running, men's golf, men's soccer, women's softball, men's and women's swimming and diving, men's and women's tennis and women's volleyball
$ Given: 15 awards for men totalling $26,975; 4 awards for women totalling $10,396; awards ranging up to $2,900 per year (in-state resident tuition) and $5,600 (out-of-state resident)
Deadline: Contact the department coaches
Contact: Mr. Donald R. Griggs, Director of Student Financial Aid

Francis Marion University
Florence, SC 29501-0546
(803) 661-1190
(803) 661-1240 (Athletic Department)

Description: Athletic scholarships for undergraduates
Restrictions: Limited to scholarships for men's baseball, men's and women's basketball, men's golf, men's soccer, men's and women's tennis, men's track and field and women's volleyball
$ Given: Unspecified number of available awards for men and women ranging from partial to full scholarships of $2,800 (tuition)
Deadline: Contact the department coaches
Contact: Mr. Scott Brown, Director of Financial Assistance

Furman University
Greenville, SC 29613
(803) 294-2204
(Financial Aid)
(803) 294-2163
(Athletic Department)

Description: Athletic scholarships for undergraduates
Restrictions: Limited to scholarships for men's and women's basketball, men's cross-country running, men's football, men's and women's golf, women's softball, men's and women's tennis, men's track and field and women's volleyball
$ Given: 90 awards for men, 36 awards for women; awards ranging up to full tuition of $16,500 per year
Deadline: Contact the department coaches
Contact: John Burns, Assistant Athletic Director

Lander College
Greenwood, SC 29649-2009
(803) 229-8340
(803) 229-8314 (Athletic
Department)

Description: Athletic scholarships for undergraduates
Restrictions: Limited to scholarships for men's and women's basketball, men's and women's cross-country running, men's soccer, women's softball and men's and women's tennis
$ Given: 15 awards for men totalling $36,000; 11 awards for women totalling $17,000; ranging up to $2,860 (in-state resident tuition) - $4,060 (out-of-state resident tuition)
Deadline: December 1. Contact the department coaches
Contact: Coach Horn, Athletic Director

Presbyterian College
Clinton, SC 29325
(803) 833-8288

Description: Athletic scholarships for undergraduates
Restrictions: Limited to scholarships for men's baseball, men's and women's basketball, men's football, men's and women's soccer, men's and women's tennis and women's volleyball
$ Given: 36 awards for men and women of various amounts ranging up to $7,500 (one-half tuition)
Deadline: Contact the department coaches
Contact: Ms. Janice Noffz, Administrative Assistant

FREE MONEY FOR ATHLETIC SCHOLARSHIPS

South Carolina State University
Wilkinson Hall
Post Office Box 1886
Orangeburg, SC 29117
(803) 536-7067
(Financial Aid)
(803) 536-8712
(Athletic Director)

Description: Athletic scholarships for undergraduates
Restrictions: Limited to scholarships for men's and women's basketball, men's cross-country running, men's football, men's golf, men's and women's tennis, men's and women's track and field, women's volleyball and men's wrestling
$ Given: Unspecified number of available awards for men and women ranging up to $5,486 (in-state resident tuition) and $7,966 (out-of-state resident tuition)
Deadline: Contact the department coaches
Contact: Mrs. Johnson, Athletic Director

University of South Carolina
1714 College Street
Columbia, SC 29208
(803) 777-8134 (Financial Aid Office)
(803) 777-4202 (Athletic Department)

Description: Athletic scholarships for undergraduates
Restrictions: Limited to scholarships for men's baseball, men's and women's basketball, men's and women's cross-country running, men's football, men's and women's golf, men's soccer, women's softball, men's and women's swimming and diving, men's and women's tennis, men's track and field and women's volleyball
$ Given: 70 awards for men and women totalling $372,534 and ranging $200 - $5,000 per year
Deadline: June. Contact the department coaches
Contact: Mr. Timothy S. Rice, Financial Aid Program Coordinator, or Mr. Mike McGee, Athletic Director

University of South Carolina - Aiken
Aiken, SC 29801
(803) 648-6851 Ext. 144

Description: Athletic scholarships for undergraduates
Restrictions: Limited to scholarships for men's baseball, men's and women's basketball, men's and women's cross-country running, men's golf, men's soccer, women's softball and men's volleyball
$ Given: Unspecified number of available awards for men and women ranging up to housing ($1,590 per year) and full tuition ($1,950 in-state resident and $4,874 out-of-state resident)
Deadline: Contact the department coaches
Contact: Mrs. Debra Taussig-Boehner, Financial Aid Officer

• • • • • • • • • • • • • • • • • • • •

**University of South
Carolina - Spartanburg**
Spartanburg, SC 29303
(803) 599-2340
(Financial Aid)
(803) 599-2141
(Athletic Department)

Description: Athletic scholarships for undergraduates
Restrictions: Limited to scholarships for men's baseball, men's and women's basketball, men's cross-country running, men's soccer, women's softball, men's and women's tennis and women's volleyball
$ Given: Unspecified number of available awards for men and women ranging: $200 - $10,000 (full scholarship for basketball; tuition, room, board and utilities)
Deadline: Contact the department coaches
Contact: Ms. Donna Hawkins, Director of Financial Aid

**University of South
Carolina - Coastal
Carolina College**
Post Office Box 1954
Myrtle Beach, SC 29578
(803) 347-3161

Description: Athletic scholarships for undergraduates
Restrictions: Limited to scholarships for men's baseball, men's and women's basketball, men's and women's cross-country running, men's and women's golf, men's soccer, women's softball, men's and women's tennis and women's volleyball
$ Given: 40 awards for men and 23 awards for women ranging: $7,430 - $11,160 (full award for men's basketball)
Deadline: Early sign-in dates one year ahead. Contact the department coaches
Contact: Jess Donnelly, Associate Athletic Director

Winthrop University
119 Tillman Hall
Rock Hill, SC 29733
(803) 323-2189
(Financial Aid)
(803) 323-2129
(Athletic Department)

Description: Athletic scholarships for undergraduates
Restrictions: Limited to scholarships for men's baseball, men's and women's basketball, men's and women's cross-country running, men's and women's golf, men's soccer, women's softball, men's and women's tennis and women's volleyball
$ Given: 7 awards for men and 3 awards for women ranging $100 - $5,000 per year.
Deadline: Contact the department coaches
Contact: Steve Vacendak, Athletic Director, or Jill Dese, Academic Advisor

FREE MONEY FOR ATHLETIC SCHOLARSHIPS

• •

SOUTH DAKOTA

Augustana College
Athletic Department
Sioux Falls, SD 57197
(605) 336-5216
(605) 336-4311
(Athletic Department)

Description: Athletic scholarships for undergraduates
Restrictions: Limited to scholarships for men's and women's basketball, men's and women's cross-country running, men's football, women's softball, men's and women's track and field, women's volleyball and men's wrestling
$ Given: 60 awards for men and 24 awards for women totalling $1,081,600
Deadline: Contact the department coaches
Contact: Bill Gross, Athletic Director

Black Hills State University
Athletic Department
University Station, Box 9509
Spearfish, SD 57799-9509
(605) 642-6194

Description: Athletic scholarships for undergraduates
Restrictions: Limited to scholarships for men's and women's basketball, men's and women's cross-country running, men's football, men's and women's track and field, women's volleyball and men's wrestling
$ Given: 80 awards for men and women totalling $38,950 ranging: $100 - $5,000 per year
Deadline: Contact the department coaches
Contact: Lauren Ferré, Athletic Director

Dakota State University
Madison, SD 57042
(605) 256-5152
(Financial Aid)
(605) 256-5229
(Athletics)

Description: Athletic scholarships for undergraduates
Restrictions: Limited to scholarships for men's and women's basketball, men's and women's cross-country running, men's football, men's and women's track and field and women's volleyball
$ Given: 14 awards for men totalling $5,670; 3 awards for women totalling $600; awards range up to $4,100 per year (tuition)
Deadline: Contact the department coaches
Contact: Ms. Sandra Paul, Financial Aid Officer

· · · · · · · · · · · · · · · · · · · ·

Northern State University
1200 South Jay Street
Aberdeen, SD 57401
(605) 622-2640
(Financial Assistance)
(605) 622-2612
(Athletic Department)

Description: Athletic scholarships for undergraduates
Restrictions: Limited to scholarships for men's and women's basketball, men's and women's cross-country running, men's football, women's golf, women's tennis, men's and women's track and field, women's volleyball and men's wrestling
$ Given: 19 awards for men totalling $8,300; 7 awards for women totalling $4,700; ranging up to full tuition of $6,000 per year (in-state resident)
Deadline: Contact the department coaches
Contact: Ms. Sharon Kienow, Director of Financial Assistance

Sioux Falls College
1501 South Prairie Avenue
Sioux Falls, SD 57105
(605) 331-6623
(Financial Aid)
(605) 331-6656
(Athletics)

Description: Athletic scholarships for undergraduates
Restrictions: Limited to scholarships for men's and women's basketball, men's and women's cross-country running, men's football, men's and women's tennis, men's and women's track and field and women's volleyball
$ Given: 29 awards for men totalling $33,400; 7 awards for women totalling $8,200 ranging: $3,000 (room and board) - $8,450 (tuition). One award of $11,450 available in each sport
Deadline: Contact the department coaches
Contact: Mr. Glen Poppinga, Director of Financial Aid, or Sid Quartermire, Athletic Director

South Dakota School of Mines and Technology
501 East SD
Rapid City, South Dakota
57701-3995
(605) 394-2416
(Dean of Students)
(605) 394-2351
(Athletic Department)

Description: Athletic scholarships for undergraduates
Restrictions: Limited to scholarships for men's and women's basketball, men's and women's cross-country running, men's football, men's and women's track and field and women's volleyball
$ Given: 65 awards for men totalling $31,900; 27 awards for women totalling $10,110; ranging up to $6,000 per year (in-state resident tuition). Average award is $1,000 per year for men and $500 per year for women
Deadline: Contact the department coaches
Contact: Dr. Howard Peterson, Dean of Students, or Irv Mondt, Athletic Director

· ·

South Dakota State University
Administration 106
Brookings, SD 57007
(605) 688-4703

Description: Athletic scholarships for undergraduates
Restrictions: Limited to scholarships for men's and women's basketball, men's and women's cross-country running, men's football, men's and women's track and field, women's volleyball and men's wrestling
$ Given: 29 awards for men totalling $67,260 and 15 awards for women totalling $25,250; partial to full scholarships
Deadline: Contact the department coaches
Contact: Fred Oine, Athletic Director

University of South Dakota
Vermillion, SD 57069-2390
(605) 677-5011
(605) 677-5309 (Athletic Department)

Description: Athletic scholarships for undergraduates
Restrictions: Limited to scholarships for men's baseball, men's and women's basketball, men's and women's cross-country running, men's football, women's softball, men's and women's swimming and diving, men's and women's tennis, men's and women's track and field and women's volleyball
$ Given: Unspecified number of available awards for men and women ranging from partial to full awards ($200 - $6,500)
Deadline: Contact the department coaches
Contact: Mary Moch, Assistant Athletic Director

TENNESSEE

Austin Peay State University
Clarksville, TN 37044
(615) 648-7907
(615) 648-6199 (Athletics)

Description: Athletic scholarships for undergraduates
Restrictions: Limited to scholarships for men's baseball, men's and women's basketball, men's and women's cross-country running, women's fast-pitch softball, men's football, men's golf, men's and women's tennis, men's and women's track and field and women's volleyball
$ Given: 120 awards for men and women ranging up to full $8,000 awards for tuition, books, registration, medical plan and board
Deadline: Contact the department coaches
Contact: Brenda Burney, Student Financial Aid Office, or Glenda Chassin, Athletics Department Administrator

Belmont University

1900 Belmont Boulevard
Nashville, TN 37212
(615) 385-6403

Description: Athletic scholarships for undergraduates
Restrictions: Limited to scholarships for men's and women's basketball, men's cross-country running and men's and women's tennis
$ Given: Unspecified number of available awards for men and women; of various amounts
Deadline: Contact the department coaches
Contact: Mr. Claude O. Pressnell, Director of Student Financial Aid, or Kenneth Sidwell, Athletic Department

Carson-Newman College

Jefferson City, TN 37760
(615) 475-9061
(615) 471-3466
(Athletic Department)

Description: Athletic scholarships for undergraduates
Restrictions: Limited to scholarships for men's baseball, men's and women's basketball, men's and women's cross-country running, men's football, men's golf, men's and women's soccer, men's and women's tennis, men's and women's track and field, women's volleyball and men's wrestling
$ Given: 45 awards for men totalling $520,490 including 25 for football (full scholarships of $10,800 per year); 23 available awards for women totalling $132,250
Deadline: Contact the department coaches
Contact: Mr. Don Elia, Director of Financial Aid, or Jerry Blalock, Compliance Officer, NCAA

Christian Brothers University

Memphis, TN 38104
(901) 722-0210 (Admissions)

Description: Athletic scholarships for undergraduates
Restrictions: Limited to scholarships for men's baseball, men's and women's basketball, men's and women's soccer and women's volleyball
$ Given: 21 awards for men and women ranging up to $12,000 per year for tuition (9 full scholarships in basketball)
Deadline: Contact the department coaches
Contact: Mr. Steve Pochard, Dean of Admissions

FREE MONEY FOR ATHLETIC SCHOLARSHIPS

• •

David Lipscomb University
3901 Granny White Pike
Nashville, TN 37204-3901
(615) 269-1776 Ext. 1795
(Athletics Department)
(800) 333-4358

Description: Athletic scholarships for undergraduates
Restrictions: Limited to scholarships for men's and women's baseball, men's and women's basketball, men's cross-country running, men's golf, men's soccer, men's and women's tennis and women's volleyball
$ Given: 25 available awards for men totalling $114,538; 8 available awards for women totalling $25,465; awards of varying amounts ranging from partial to full scholarships of $13,000 per year for baseball and basketball
Deadline: Contact the department coaches
Contact: Mr. Steve Davidson, Director of Financial Aid, or Mrs. Phillips, Athletics Office

East Tennessee State University
Box 24160A
Johnson City, TN 37614
(615) 929-4313
(615) 929-6119 (Athletic Department)

Description: Athletic scholarships for undergraduates
Restrictions: Limited to scholarships for men's and women's baseball, men's and women's basketball, men's and women's cross-country running, men's football, men's and women's tennis, men's and women's track and field and women's volleyball
$ Given: 12 available awards for men totalling $96,000; 12 available awards for women totalling $96,000; awards ranging up to full tuition of $8,000 per year
Deadline: Contact the department coaches
Contact: Ms. Linda Clemons, Director of Financial Aid

Freed-Hardeman University
Henderson, TN 38340
(901) 989-6663
(901) 989-6042 (Athletics)

Description: Athletic scholarships for undergraduates
Restrictions: Limited to scholarships for men's baseball, men's and women's basketball, men's golf, women's softball, men's and women's tennis and women's volleyball
$ Given: 12 awards for men totalling $44,000; 6 awards for women; awards ranging from partial to full scholarships of $9,000 per year for tuition (full awards for baseball and basketball)
Deadline: Contact the department coaches
Contact: Mr. Charlie Smith, Chairman, Athletic Department

. . . .

Lee College
Cleveland, TN 37311
(615) 472-2111 Ext. 330
(Financial Aid)
Ext. 061
(Athletic Department)

Description: Athletic scholarships for undergraduates
Restrictions: Limited to scholarships for men's and women's basketball, men's golf, men's and women's soccer, women's softball, men's and women's tennis and women's volleyball
$ Given: Available awards for men and women ranging up to full scholarships of $8,300 per year
Deadline: Contact the department coaches
Contact: Mr. Michael Ellis, Director of Student Financial Aid

Lincoln Memorial University
Harrogate, TN 37752
(615) 869-3611

Description: Athletic scholarships for undergraduates
Restrictions: Limited to scholarships for men's baseball, men's and women's basketball, men's and women's cross-country running, men's golf, men's and women's soccer (women's in 1994), women's softball, men's and women's tennis and women's volleyball
$ Given: Unspecified number of available awards for men and women ranging $500 - $5,400 per year (full tuition)
Deadline: Contact the department coaches
Contact: Ms. Patricia G. Peace, Director of Financial Aid

Memphis State University
Memphis, TN 38152
(901) 678-2303
(901) 678-2335 (Athletics)

Description: Athletic scholarships for undergraduates
Restrictions: Limited to scholarships for men's baseball, men's and women's basketball, men's football, men's and women's golf, men's soccer, men's and women's tennis, men's and women's track and field and women's volleyball
$ Given: 71 awards for men and women ranging: $200 (books) - $1,830 per year (in-state resident tuition) and $5,612 per year (out-of-state resident tuition); basketball and football offer full awards
Deadline: Contact the department coaches
Contact: Mr. Allen J. Hammond, Director of Student Aid, or Sally Andrews, Compliance Officer

FREE MONEY FOR ATHLETIC SCHOLARSHIPS

• •

Tennessee State University
Nashville, TN 37209-1561
(615) 320-3750
(Financial Aid)
(615) 320-3596
(Athletic Department)
(615) 320-3054
(Compliance Officer)

Description: Athletic scholarships for undergraduates
Restrictions: Limited to scholarships for men's and women's basketball, men's football, men's golf, men's and women's tennis and men's and women's track and field
$ Given: 64 awards for men and 14 awards for women ranging up to full awards for football and basketball: $4,300 (in-state resident) and $8,100 (out-of-state resident)
Deadline: Contact the department coaches
Contact: William Thomas, Athletic Director, or Wayne Bill, Compliance Officer

Tennessee Technological University
Box 5006
Cookeville, TN 38505
(615) 372-3888 (Admissions)
(615) 372-3949 (Athletic Department)

Description: Athletic scholarships for undergraduates
Restrictions: Limited to scholarships for men's baseball, men's and women's basketball, men's and women's cross-country, men's football, men's and women's golf, men's and women's riflery, women's softball, men's and women's tennis, women's track and women's volleyball
$ Given: 104 awards for men totalling $531,789 and 41 awards for women; of various amounts ranging up to full scholarships
Deadline: Contact the department coaches
Contact: Dr. Larimore, Athletic Director, or Marcia Borys, Assistant Athletic Director

Union University
Jackson, TN 38305
(901) 668-1818 Ext. 211
(901) 661-5130
(Athletic Department)

Description: Athletic scholarships for undergraduates
Restrictions: Limited to scholarships for men's baseball, men's and women's basketball, men's golf and men's and women's tennis
$ Given: Unspecified number of available awards for men and women ranging up to $9,000 (full scholarships for tuition)
Deadline: Contact the department coaches
Contact: Mr. Don Morris, Assistant Vice President/Director of Financial Aid, or Coach Blackstock, Athletic Director

• •

University of Tennessee - Chattanooga
Chattanooga, TN 37403
(615) 755-4677
(Financial Aid)
(615) 755-4583
(Athletic Department)

Description: Athletic scholarships for undergraduates
Restrictions: Limited to scholarships for men's and women's basketball, men's and women's cross-country running, men's football, men's golf, women's softball, men's and women's tennis, men's and women's track, women's volleyball and men's wrestling
$ Given: Unspecified number of available awards for men and women ranging $800 - $10,000
Deadline: Contact the department coaches
Contact: Mary Tinkler, Academic Advisor for Athletics

University of Tennessee - Martin
Martin, TN 38238
(901) 587-7660
(Men's Athletics)
(901) 587-7680
(Women's Athletics)

Description: Athletic scholarships for undergraduates
Restrictions: Limited to scholarships for men's and women's basketball, men's and women's cross-country, men's football, men's golf, men's and women's riflery, men's and women's tennis, men's and women's track and women's volleyball
$ Given: Unspecified number of available awards for men and women ranging: $200 - $8,000 per year (full scholarship)
Deadline: Contact the department coaches
Contact: Coach Kernel Kaler, Athletic Director

University of Tennessee - Knoxville
115 Student Services Building
Knoxville, TN 37996-0210
(615) 974-3131
(615) 974-1224
(Men's Athletic Department)
(615) 974-0001 (Women's Athletic Department)

Description: Athletic scholarships for undergraduates
Restrictions: Limited to scholarships for men's and women's basketball, men's and women's cross-country running, men's football, men's golf, men's and women's swimming and diving, men's and women's tennis, men's and women's track and field and women's volleyball
$ Given: 155 available awards for men and 75 available awards for women ranging: $200 - $9,000
Deadline: Contact the department coaches
Contact: Malcolm McGinnis, Compliance Officer/Associate Athletic Director

• •

Vanderbilt University
401 24th Avenue South
Nashville, TN 37212
(615) 322-2561 (Admissions)
(615) 322-4727 (Athletics)

Description: Athletic scholarships for undergraduates
Restrictions: Limited to scholarships for men's and women's basketball, women's cross-country running, men's football, men's and women's golf, men's and women's soccer, women's swimming and diving and men's and women's tennis
$ Given: 41 awards for men totalling $687,309 and 13 awards for women totalling $167,715; ranging up to full scholarships of $25,000 per year
Deadline: Contact the department coaches
Contact: Paul Hollahan, Athletic Director

TEXAS

Abilene Christian University
ACU Station, Box 8480
Abilene, TX 79699
(915) 674-2330

Description: Athletic scholarships for undergraduates
Restrictions: Limited to scholarships for men's baseball, men's and women's basketball, men's and women's cross-country running, men's football, men's golf, men's and women's tennis, men's and women's track and field and women's volleyball
$ Given: 26 awards for men and 15 awards for women; average grants ranging up to $11,000 per year
Deadline: Contact the department coach, Todd McKnight
Contact: Mr. Gene Linder, Assistant Vice President of Admissions, Scholarships and Financial Aid

Angelo State University
Athletic Department
San Angelo, TX 76909
(915) 942-2091

Description: Athletic scholarships for undergraduates
Restrictions: Limited to scholarships for men's and women's basketball, men's and women's cross-country running, men's football, men's and women's track and field and women's volleyball
$ Given: Unspecified number of awards ranging $2,000 - half-tuition
Deadline: Contact the department coaches
Contact: Mr. James B. Parker, Director of Financial Aid, or Mr. Vandergriff, Athletics Department

Baylor University
Post Office Box 97028
Waco, TX 76798-7028
(817) 755-2611
(817) 755-1234 (Athletics
Department)

Description: Athletic scholarships for undergraduates
Restrictions: Limited to scholarships for men's baseball, men's and women's basketball, men's and women's cross-country running, men's football, men's and women's golf, men's and women's tennis, men's and women's track and field, women's volleyball
$ Given: 30 awards for men and 14 awards for women ranging up to full fees and tuition of $10,000
Deadline: Contact the department coaches
Contact: Tom Hill, Athletic Department

East Texas State University
Commerce, TX 75429
(903) 886-5081

Description: Athletic scholarships for undergraduates
Restrictions: Limited to scholarships for men's and women's basketball, men's and women's cross-country running, men's football, men's golf, men's and women's track and field and women's volleyball
$ Given: 125 available awards for men and women totalling $400,000; of various amounts ranging up to full tuition, room and board for a year
Deadline: Contact the department coaches
Contact: Dr. Margaret Harbison, Director of Athletics

Incarnate Word College
4301 Broadway
San Antonio, TX 78209
(512) 829-6008

Description: Athletic scholarships for undergraduates
Restrictions: Limited to scholarships for men's and women's basketball, men's and women's cross-country running, men's and women's golf, men's and women's soccer, men's and women's tennis and women's volleyball
$ Given: 6 awards for men and 17 awards for women ranging up to $8,250 (partial tuition)
Deadline: Contact the department coaches
Contact: Ms. Grace Zapata, Processing Coordinator

FREE MONEY FOR ATHLETIC SCHOLARSHIPS

• •

Lamar University - Beaumont
Beaumont, TX 77705
(409) 880-8450
(Financial Aid)
(409) 880-8332
(Athletic Department)

Description: Athletic scholarships for undergraduates
Restrictions: Limited to scholarships for men's baseball, men's and women's basketball, men's and women's cross-country running, men's and women's golf, men's and women's tennis, men's and women's track and field and women's volleyball
$ Given: 45 available awards for men totalling and 45 available awards for women ranging up to $5,000 per year (in-state resident tuition)
Deadline: Contact the department coaches
Contact: Mrs. Ralynn Castete, Director of Financial Aid, or Paul Zeck, Athletics Department

Midwestern State University
3400 Taft Boulevard
Wichita Falls, TX 76308
(817) 692-6611 Ext. 4328

Description: Athletic scholarships for undergraduates
Restrictions: Limited to scholarships for men's and women's basketball and men's soccer
$ Given: 8 awards for men totalling $6,197; 6 awards for women totalling $2,614 ranging up to $2,700 (in-state resident tuition) and $5,400 (out-of-state resident tuition)
Deadline: Contact the department coaches
Contact: Mrs. Barbara Merkle, Director of School Relations

Rice University
Post Office Box 1892
Houston, TX 77251
(713) 527-4036 (Admissions)
(713) 527-6096 (Athletics)

Description: Athletic scholarships for undergraduates
Restrictions: Limited to scholarships for men's baseball, men's and women's basketball, men's and women's cross-country running, men's football, men's golf, men's and women's swimming and diving, men's and women's tennis, men's and women's track and field and women's volleyball
$ Given: 60 awards for men and 30 awards for women; of various amounts ranging up to full tuition, room and board awards of $16,000 (25 for men's football and 26 for men's and women's basketball)
Deadline: Contact the department coaches
Contact: Mr. Ron Moss, Director of Admissions, or Barbara Tolar, Athletics

· · · · · · · · · · · · · · · · · · · ·

St. Edward's University
Austin, TX 78704
(512) 448-8480 (Athletics)
(512) 448-8500 (Admissions)

Description: Athletic scholarships for undergraduates
Restrictions: Limited to scholarships for men's baseball, men's and women's basketball, men's golf, men's and women's soccer, women's softball, men's and women's tennis and women's volleyball
$ Given: 112 available awards for men and women of various amounts ranging: $500 - $7,000 ($1,800 - $2,200 average scholarship)
Deadline: Contact the department coaches
Contact: Ms. Doris F. Constantine, Director of Financial Aid, or John Knorr, Athletic Director

St. Mary's University of San Antonio
San Antonio, TX 78228-8503
(512) 436-3141
(Financial Aid)
(512) 436-3528
(Athletic Department)

Description: Athletic scholarships for undergraduates
Restrictions: Limited to scholarships for men's and women's basketball, men's golf, men's soccer, men's and women's tennis and women's volleyball
$ Given: Unspecified number of available awards for men and women ranging up to partial tuition of $8,100 per year
Deadline: Contact the department coaches
Contact: Mr. David R. Krause, Director of Office of Financial Assistance

Sam Houston State University
Athletic Department
Post Office Box 2268
Huntsville, TX 77341
(409) 294-1724 (Financial Aid)

Description: Athletic scholarships for undergraduates
Restrictions: Limited to scholarships for men's baseball, men's and women's basketball, men's and women's cross-country, men's football, men's golf, women's softball, women's tennis, men's and women's track and women's volleyball
$ Given: 150 available awards for men and women ranging up to $7,800 (in-state resident tuition). Scholarships of $5,000 per year are available in every sport
Deadline: Contact the department coaches
Contact: Mr. Jess Davis, Director of Student Financial Aid, or Dr. Case, Athletic Director

FREE MONEY FOR ATHLETIC SCHOLARSHIPS

Southern Methodist University
Box 196
Dallas, TX 75275
(214) 768-2864
(Athletic Department)

Description: Athletic scholarships for undergraduates
Restrictions: Limited to scholarships for men's and women's basketball, men's and women's cross-country running, men's football, men's and women's golf, men's and women's soccer, men's and women's swimming and diving, men's and women's tennis and men's and women's track and field
$ Given: Unspecified number of available awards for men and women ranging: $200 - $18,000
Deadline: Contact the department coaches (recruiting season ends around May 1)
Contact: Charles Howard, Compliance and Academic Liaison Officer

Southwestern Christian College
Terrell, TX 75160
(214) 524-3341 Ext. 121
(Athletics)

Description: Athletic scholarships for undergraduates
Restrictions: Limited to scholarships for men's and women's basketball and men's track and field
$ Given: 20 available awards for men and 15 available awards for women ranging: $500 - $5,000 per year for two years
Deadline: Contact the department coaches
Contact: Seneca Mangum, Athletic Director

Southwest Texas State University
601 University Drive
San Marcos, TX 78666-4602
(512) 245-2315
(Financial Aid)
(512) 245-2114
(Athletic Department)

Description: Athletic scholarships for undergraduates
Restrictions: Limited to scholarships for men's baseball, men's and women's basketball, men's cross-country running, men's football, men's golf, women's softball, men's and women's tennis, men's and women's track and field and women's volleyball
$ Given: 10 available awards for men and 10 available awards for women ranging $1,600 - $7,000
Deadline: Contact the department coaches
Contact: Richard Hannan, Athletic Director

• •

Stephen F. Austin State University
Nacogdoches, TX 75962
(409) 568-3501
(men's athletics)
(409) 568-3506
(women's athletics)

Description: Athletic scholarships for undergraduates
Restrictions: Limited to scholarships for men's baseball, men's and women's basketball, men's and women's cross-country running, men's football, men's golf, women's softball, men's and women's track and field and women's volleyball
$ Given: Unspecified number of available awards for men and women ranging: $200 - $6,000 (in-state resident scholarship) and $11,000 (out-of-state resident scholarship)
Deadline: Contact the department coaches
Contact: Matt Findley, Compliance Officer, or Sadie Allison, Women's Athletic Director

Texas A&I University
Campus Box 115
Kingsville, TX 78363
(512) 595-3911
(Financial Aid)
(512) 595-2411
(Athletic Department)

Description: Athletic scholarships for undergraduates
Restrictions: Limited to scholarships for men's baseball, men's and women's basketball, men's and women's cross-country running, men's football and women's volleyball
$ Given: Unspecified number of available awards for men and women ranging: $200 - $10,000 (full award)
Deadline: Contact the department coaches
Contact: Ron Hans, Athletic Director

Texas A&M University
College Station, TX 77843
(409) 845-3988
(Scholarship Department)
(409) 845-4616/1159
(Athletic Departments)

Description: Athletic scholarships for undergraduates
Restrictions: Limited to scholarships for men's and women's basketball, men's and women's cross-country running, men's football, men's and women's golf, women's soccer, men's and women's swimming and diving, men's and women's tennis, men's and women's track and field and women's volleyball
$ Given: 56 awards for men totalling $168,000 and 26 awards for women totalling $65,000; of various amounts
Deadline: Contact the department coaches
Contact: Linda Rotsch, Athletic Financial Aid Coordinator, or John Thornton, Assistant to the Athletic Director

FREE MONEY FOR ATHLETIC SCHOLARSHIPS

• • • • • • • • • • • • • • • • • • • •

Texas Christian University
Post Office Box 30787
Fort Worth, TX 76129
(817) 921-7951/7965
(Athletic Department)

Description: Athletic scholarships for undergraduates
Restrictions: Limited to scholarships for men's baseball, men's and women's basketball, men's and women's cross-country running, men's football, men's and women's golf, men's and women's swimming and diving, men's and women's tennis and men's and women's track and field
$ Given: Unspecified number of available awards for men and women ranging: $1,000 - $14,500 (full awards in basketball and football)
Deadline: Contact the department coaches by October of senior high school year
Contact: Carolyn Dixon, Athletic Director

Texas Southern University
Houston, TX 77004
(713) 527-7245/7271
(Athletic Department)

Description: Athletic scholarships for undergraduates
Restrictions: Limited to scholarships for men's baseball, men's and women's basketball, men's and women's cross-country running, men's football, men's and women's golf, men's and women's tennis, men's and women's track and field and women's volleyball
$ Given: 300 available awards for men and women ranging: $200 - $8,000 per year
Deadline: Contact the department coaches
Contact: Dr. Curtis Williams, Athletic Director

Texas Tech University
Athletic Department
Post Office Box 43021
Lubbock, TX 79409-3021
(806) 742-3426
(Financial Aid)
(806) 742-3355
(Athletic Department)

Description: Athletic scholarships for undergraduates
Restrictions: Limited to scholarships for men's baseball, men's and women's basketball, men's and women's cross-country, men's football, men's and women's golf, men's and women's tennis, men's and women's track and women's volleyball
$ Given: Unspecified number of available awards for men and women ranging: $200 - $10,000 (partial to full)
Deadline: Contact the department coaches
Contact: Edna Petty, Administrative Assistant, Athletics

Texas Woman's University
Post Office Box 22628
Denton, TX 76204-0909
(817) 898-3050
(817) 898-2378
(Athletic Department)

Description: Athletic scholarships for undergraduates
Restrictions: Limited to scholarships for women's basketball, women's gymnastics, women's tennis and women's volleyball
$ Given: Unspecified number of available awards for men and women ranging $200 - $5,000 per year
Deadline: Contact the department coaches
Contact: Judy Sonthard, Athletic Director

University of North Texas
Denton, TX 76203
(817) 565-2016
(Financial Aid)
(817) 565-2662
(Athletic Department)

Description: Athletic scholarships for undergraduates
Restrictions: Limited to scholarships for men's and women's basketball, men's and women's cross-country running, men's football, men's and women's golf, men's soccer, men's and women's tennis, men's and women's track and field and women's volleyball
$ Given: 100 available awards for men and 40 available awards for women ranging $200 - $5,000 (in-state resident) and $9,000 (out-of-state resident)
Deadline: June 15. Contact the department coaches
Contact: George Young, Assistant Athletic Director

University of Texas - Arlington
Post Office Box 19199
Arlington, TX 76019
(817) 273-2197
(Scholarship Office)
(817) 273-2261
(Athletic Department)

Description: Athletic scholarships for undergraduates
Restrictions: Limited to scholarships for men's baseball, men's and women's basketball, men's and women's cross-country running, men's golf, women's softball, men's and women's tennis, men's and women's track and field and women's volleyball
$ Given: 17 awards for men totalling $48,855 and 13 awards for women totalling $39,043; awards range up to full scholarships of $5,500 (in-state residents) and $10,000 (out-of-state residents)
Deadline: Signing periods April 14 - May 15. Contact the department coaches
Contact: Coach Skelton, Athletic Director

FREE MONEY FOR ATHLETIC SCHOLARSHIPS

. . . .

**University of Texas -
Austin**
Post Office Box 7758
Utah Station
Austin, TX 78712
(512) 471-4602
(Athletic Department)

Description: Athletic scholarships for undergraduates
Restrictions: Limited to scholarships for men's baseball, men's and women's basketball, men's and women's cross-country running, men's football, men's and women's golf, men's and women's swimming and diving, men's and women's tennis, men's and women's track and field and women's volleyball
$ Given: 75 available awards for men and 40 available awards for women ranging: $200 - $12,000 per year
Deadline: Contact the department coaches
Contact: Mr. Dodds, Athletic Director

**University of Texas -
El Paso**
El Paso, TX 79968
(915) 747-5890
(Recruiting & Scholarships)
(915) 747-5347
(Athletic Department)

Description: Athletic scholarships for undergraduates
Restrictions: Limited to scholarships for men's and women's basketball, men's and women's cross-country running, men's football, men's and women's golf, women's tennis, men's and women's track and field and women's volleyball
$ Given: 31 awards for men totalling $47,687 and 12 awards for women totalling $18,459; awards ranging: $200 - $6,000 (full scholarship for in-state resident) and $10,000 (full scholarship for out-of-state resident)
Deadline: Contact the department coaches
Contact: Brad Hovious, Athletic Director

**University of Texas -
San Antonio**
6900 North Loop 1604 West
San Antonio, TX 78249
(210) 691-4599 (Admissions)
(210) 691-4444
(Athletic Director)

Description: Athletic scholarships for undergraduates
Restrictions: Limited to scholarships for men's baseball, men's and women's basketball, men's and women's cross-country running, men's golf, women's softball, men's and women's tennis, men's and women's track and field and women's volleyball
$ Given: 42 awards for men totalling $37,009 and 44 awards for women totalling $43,694; awards range $1,800 - $8,000 (full scholarship for in-state resident) and $12,000 (full scholarship for out-of-state resident)
Deadline: August 1. Contact the department coaches
Contact: Bobby Thompson, Athletic Director

. . . .

University of Texas - Pan American

1201 West University Drive
Edinburg, TX 78539
(210) 381-2509
(Financial Aid)
(210) 381-2220
(Athletic Department)

Description: Athletic scholarships for undergraduates
Restrictions: Limited to scholarships for men's and women's basketball, men's and women's cross-country running, men's and women's golf, men's soccer, men's and women's tennis, men's and women's track and field and women's volleyball
$ Given: 21 awards for men and 12 available awards for women ranging: $200 - $6,000 (full scholarship for in-state residents) and $10,000 (full scholarship for out-of-state residents)
Deadline: Contact the department coaches
Contact: Gary Gallup, Athletic Director

West Texas State University

Canyon, TX 79016
(806) 656-2055
(Financial Aid)
(806) 656-2040
(Athletic Department)

Description: Athletic scholarships for undergraduates
Restrictions: Limited to scholarships for men's and women's basketball, cheerleading, men's soccer, men's and women's tennis and women's volleyball
$ Given: 25 available awards for men and 25 available awards for women ranging up to full scholarships of $4,162 (in-state resident) and $8,302 (out-of-state resident). Partial scholarships only for men's soccer.
Deadline: Contact the department coaches
Contact: Mike Chandler, Athletic Director

UTAH

Brigham Young University

A-41 Abraham Smoot Building
Provo, UT 84602
(801) 378-4104
(801) 378-3251 (Athletics)

Description: Athletic scholarships for undergraduates
Restrictions: Limited to scholarships for men's baseball, men's and women's basketball, men's and women's cross-country running, men's football, men's and women's golf, men's and women's gymnastics, men's and women's swimming and diving, men's and women's tennis, men's and women's track and field, men's and women's volleyball and men's wrestling
$ Given: 180 available awards for men including full scholarships for basketball (15 awards) and football (92 awards); 60 available awards for women; ranging $5,760 - $7,612
Deadline: Contact the department coaches
Contact: Mr. Duane L. Bartle, Scholarship Coordinator

FREE MONEY FOR ATHLETIC SCHOLARSHIPS

• •

Southern Utah University
Cedar City, UT 84720
(801) 586-7735
(Financial Aid)
(801) 586-1937
(Athletic Department)

Description: Athletic scholarships for undergraduates
Restrictions: Limited to scholarships for men's baseball, men's and women's basketball, men's cross-country running, men's football, men's golf, women's gymnastics, women's softball and men's and women's track and field
$ Given: Unspecified number of available awards for men and women ranging: $200 - $1,600 per year (out-of-state resident) and $200 - $5,000 per year (in-state resident)
Deadline: Contact the department coaches
Contact: Jack Bishop, Athletic Director

University of Utah
Salt Lake City, UT 84112
(801) 581-6211
(Financial Aid)
(801) 581-8171
(Athletic Department)

Description: Athletic scholarships for undergraduates
Restrictions: Limited to scholarships for men's and women's basketball, men's and women's cross-country running, men's football, men's golf, women's gymnastics, men's and women's cross-country skiing, men's and women's downhill skiing, women's softball, men's and women's swimming and diving, men's and women's tennis, men's and women's track and field, women's volleyball and men's water polo
$ Given: 66 awards for men and 30 awards for women ranging up to full tuition of $7,000 per year (in-state resident) and $9,000 per year (out-of-state resident)
Deadline: Contact the department coaches
Contact: Mr. Harold R. Weight, Director of Financial Aid

Utah State University
Logan, UT 84322
(801) 750-1021
(801) 750-1850
(Athletic Department)

Description: Athletic scholarships for undergraduates
Restrictions: Limited to scholarships for men's basketball, men's and women's cross-country running, men's football, men's golf, women's gymnastics, women's softball, men's and women's tennis, men's and women's track and field and women's volleyball
$ Given: Unspecified number of available awards for men and women ranging: $1,800 - full scholarships of $6,000 (in-state resident) and $10,000 (out-of-state resident)
Deadline: Contact the department coaches
Contact: Kaye Hart, Associate Athletic Director

- - - - - - - - - - - - - - - - - - - -

Weber State University
Ogden, UT 84408-1017
(801) 626-6585
(Financial Aid)
(801) 626-2706
(Athletic Department)

Description: Athletic scholarships for undergraduates
Restrictions: Limited to scholarships for men's and women's basketball, men's and women's cross-country running, men's football, men's golf, men's and women's tennis, men's and women's track and field and women's volleyball
$ Given: Unspecified number of available awards for men and women ranging up to full scholarships of $8,000 per year (partial scholarships for golf, tennis and track)
Deadline: Contact the department coaches
Contact: Rick Ordyna, Assistant Athletic Director, or Carol Nelson, Woman's Senior Administrator

VERMONT

Saint Michael's College
Colchester, VT 05439
(802) 654-2379
(Financial Aid)
(802) 654-2500
(Athletic Department)

Description: Athletic scholarships for undergraduates
Restrictions: Limited to scholarships for men's and women's basketball
$ Given: 11 awards for men totalling $198,330 and 11 awards for women totalling $198,330; ranging up to full tuition of $18,030 per year
Deadline: Contact the department coaches
Contact: Edward Markey, Athletic Director

University of Vermont
330 Waterman
South Prospect Street
Burlington, VT 05405
(802) 656-3156
(Financial Aid)
(802) 656-3074
(Athletic Department)

Description: Athletic scholarships for undergraduates
Restrictions: Limited to scholarships for men's and women's alpine skiing, men's baseball, men's and women's basketball, women's cross-country running, men's and women's cross-country skiing, men's and women's downhill skiing, women's field hockey, women's gymnastics, men's ice hockey, women's lacrosse, men's and women's soccer, women's swimming, women's tennis, women's track and field and women's volleyball
$ Given: Ranging $200 - $18,000 per year. Full scholarships given in most sports, especially basketball, ice hockey and skiing.
Deadline: Contact the department coaches by February 1
Contact: Richard Farnham, Athletic Director

FREE MONEY FOR ATHLETIC SCHOLARSHIPS

. . . .

VIRGINIA

Clinch Valley College of the University of Virginia
College Avenue
Wise, VA 24293
(703) 328-0140
(703) 328-0206
(Athletic Department)

Description: Athletic scholarships for undergraduates
Restrictions: Limited to scholarships for men's baseball, men's and women's basketball and men's and women's tennis
$ Given: Unspecified number of available awards for men totalling $24,000 and women totalling $16,000; awards ranging up to $6,200 per year (tuition)
Deadline: Contact the department coaches
Contact: Ms. Sheila Cox, Director of Student Financial Aid

College of William and Mary
Williamsburg, VA 23185
(804) 221-4223
(804) 221-3400
(Athletic Department)

Description: Athletic scholarships for undergraduates
Restrictions: Limited to scholarships for men's and women's basketball, men's and women's cross-country, women's field hockey, men's football, men's and women's golf, men's and women's gymnastics, women's lacrosse, men's and women's soccer, women's swimming and diving, men's and women's tennis, men's and women's track and field, women's volleyball and men's wrestling
$ Given: Approximately 41 awards for men and 25 awards for women; ranging up to $7,000 per year (tuition)
Deadline: Contact the department coaches
Contact: Dr. Jean A. Scott, Dean of Admission

George Mason University
Fairfax, VA 22030
(703) 993-2349
(703) 993-3282
(Athletic Department)

Description: Athletic scholarships for undergraduates
Restrictions: Limited to scholarships for men's baseball, men's and women's basketball, men's and women's cross-country running, men's golf, men's and women's riflery, men's and women's soccer, women's softball, men's and women's tennis, men's and women's track and field, men's and women's volleyball and men's wrestling
$ Given: Unspecified number of available awards for men and women ranging up to $3,840 (tuition, in-state residents) and $10,080 (out-of-state residents)
Deadline: Contact the department coaches
Contact: Susan Collins, Associate Athletic Director

• • • • • • • • • • • • • • • • • • • •

Hampton University
Hampton, VA 23668
(804) 727-5332
(Financial Aid)
(804) 727-5641 (Athletics)

Description: Athletic scholarships for undergraduates
Restrictions: Limited to scholarships for men's and women's basketball, men's and women's cross-country running, men's football, men's tennis, men's and women's track and field, women's volleyball and men's wrestling
$ Given: Unspecified number of available awards for men and women ranging up to $10,000 per year
Deadline: Contact the department coaches
Contact: Mrs. Veronica Finch, Director of Financial Aid

James Madison University
Harrisonburg, VA 22807
(703) 568-6644
(Financial Aid)
(703) 568-6164
(Athletic Department)

Description: Athletic scholarships for undergraduates
Restrictions: Limited to scholarships for men's baseball, men's and women's basketball, men's and women's cross-country running, men's football, men's and women's golf, men's and women's gymnastics, women's lacrosse, men's and women's soccer, men's and women's swimming and diving, men's and women's tennis, men's and women's track and field, women's volleyball and men's wrestling
$ Given: Unspecified number of available awards for men and women ranging $3,798 (in-state resident tuition) - $7,650 (out-of-state resident tuition)
Deadline: Contact the department coaches
Contact: Mr. John H. Sellers, Director of Financial Aid

Liberty University
Lynchburg, VA 24506-8001
(804) 582-2270

Description: Athletic scholarships for undergraduates
Restrictions: Limited to scholarships for men's baseball, men's and women's basketball, men's and women's cross-country running, men's football, men's golf, men's soccer, men's tennis, men's and women's track and field, women's volleyball and men's wrestling
$ Given: 30 awards for men and 9 awards for women ranging: $500 - $10,000 (full tuition scholarships)
Deadline: Contact the department coaches
Contact: Mr. Norman J. Westervelt, Director of Student Financial Aid

FREE MONEY FOR ATHLETIC SCHOLARSHIPS

• •

Longwood College
Farmville, VA 23901
(804) 395-2060 (Admissions)
(804) 395-2057
(Athletic Department)

Description: Athletic scholarships for undergraduates
Restrictions: Limited to scholarships for men's baseball, men's and women's basketball, women's field hockey, men's and women's golf, men's soccer, women's tennis and men's wrestling
$ Given: 15 awards for men totalling $32,100; 7 awards for women totalling $19,523 ranging up to $7,800 (in-state resident tuition, room and board) and $12,884 (out-of-state resident tuition, room and board)
Deadline: Contact the department coaches
Contact: Mr. Bob Chonko, Director of Admissions

Norfolk State University
Norfolk, VA 23504
(804) 683-8381
(Financial Aid)
(804) 683-8152
(Athletic Department)

Description: Athletic scholarships for undergraduates
Restrictions: Limited to scholarships for men's baseball, men's and women's basketball, men's cross-country running, men's football, women's softball, women's track and field, women's volleyball and men's wrestling
$ Given: 203 awards for men and women ranging up to $6,100 full tuition (in-state resident) and $10,000 (out-of-state resident)
Deadline: Contact the department coaches
Contact: William Price, Athletic Director

Old Dominion University
Student Financial Aid Office
126 Old Administration
Building
Norfolk, VA 23529-0052
(804) 683-3683
(Financial Aid)
(804) 683-3372
(Athletic Department)

Description: Athletic scholarships for undergraduates
Restrictions: Limited to scholarships for men's baseball, men's and women's basketball, men's and women's cross-country running, women's field hockey, men's golf, women's lacrosse, men's and women's soccer, men's and women's swimming and diving, men's and women's tennis and men's wrestling
$ Given: 25 awards for men totalling $116,440; 17 awards for women totalling $103,187; awards ranging: $550 (books) - $4,000 (tuition, room and board)
Deadline: Contact the department coaches
Contact: Dr. Jim Jarrett, Athletic Director, or Mikki Flowers, Scholarship Coordinator

• • • • • • • • • • • • • • • • • • • •

Radford University
Radford, VA 24142
(703) 831-5408

Description: Athletic scholarships for undergraduates
Restrictions: Limited to scholarships for men's baseball, men's and women's basketball, men's and women's cross-country running, women's field hockey, men's golf, men's and women's gymnastics, men's lacrosse, men's and women's soccer, women's softball, men's and women's tennis and women's volleyball
$ Given: 16 awards for men totalling $41,626; 11 awards for women totalling $38,000
Deadline: Contact the department coaches
Contact: Mr. H. S. Johnston Jr., Director of Financial Aid

University of Richmond
Sarah Brunet Hall
University of Richmond, VA 23173
(804) 289-8438
(Financial Aid)
(804) 289-8371
(Athletic Department)

Description: Athletic scholarships for undergraduates
Restrictions: Limited to scholarships for men's baseball, men's and women's basketball, women's field hockey, men's football, men's golf, women's lacrosse, men's soccer, men's and women's swimming and diving and men's and women's tennis
$ Given: 35 awards for men and women totalling $324,950; of various amounts ranging up to full tuition and board
Deadline: Contact the department coaches
Contact: Ms. Cynthia B. Long, Associate Director of Financial Aid, or Chuck Boone, Athletic Director

University of Virginia
Post Office Box Box 9021
Charlottesville, VA 22906
(804) 924-3725
(804) 982-5000
(Athletic Department)

Description: Athletic scholarships for undergraduates
Restrictions: Limited to scholarships for men's baseball, men's and women's basketball, men's and women's cross-country running, men's football, men's golf, men's and women's lacrosse, men's and women's soccer, women's softball, men's and women's swimming and diving, men's and women's tennis, men's and women's track and field, women's volleyball and men's wrestling
$ Given: 48 awards for men totalling $394,852 and 21 awards for women totalling $139,237; of various amounts ranging from partial to full tuition
Deadline: Contact the department coaches
Contact: Mr. James W. Ramsey Jr., Associate Director of Financial Aid

FREE MONEY FOR ATHLETIC SCHOLARSHIPS

• • • • • • • • • • • • • • • • • •

Virginia Commonwealth University
327 West Main Street
Richmond, VA 23284
(804) 367-1277
(Athletic Department)

Description: Athletic scholarships for undergraduates
Restrictions: Limited to scholarships for men's baseball, men's and women's basketball, men's and women's cross-country running, women's field hockey, men's golf, men's soccer, men's and women's tennis, men's and women's track and field and women's volleyball
$ Given: Unspecified number of awards ranging $200 - $13,000 per year
Deadline: After June 1 for the 1994-95 school year. Contact the department coaches
Contact: Mr. Horace Wooldridge, Director of Admission, or Alfreeda Goff, Associate Athletic Director

Virginia Polytechnic Institute and State University
104 Burruss Hall
Blacksburg, VA 24061-0222
(703) 231-6267 (Admissions)
(703) 231-6796
(Athletic Department)
(703) 231-5497
(Compliance Officer)

Description: Athletic scholarships for undergraduates
Restrictions: Limited to scholarships for men's baseball, men's and women's basketball, men's and women's cross-country running, men's football, men's golf, men's and women's soccer, men's and women's swimming and diving, men's and women's tennis, men's and women's track and field, women's volleyball and men's wrestling
$ Given: 48 awards for men and 16 awards for women ranging from partial to full awards ($200 - $15,000 per year)
Deadline: Contact the department coaches
Contact: Mr. David Bousquet, Director of Undergraduate Admissions, or Steve Horton, Compliance Officer

Virginia State University
Petersburg, VA 23803
(804) 524-5600/5632
(Athletic Department)

Description: Athletic scholarships for undergraduates
Restrictions: Limited to scholarships for men's and women's basketball, men's football, men's and women's track and field and women's volleyball
$ Given: 75 available awards for men and 40 available awards for women ranging $6,000 - $7,000 (full in-state resident scholarship) and $10,050 (full out-of-state resident scholarship)
Deadline: Contact the department coaches
Contact: Coach Lewis Anderson, Athletic Director

WASHINGTON

Western Washington University
Bellingham, WA 98225
(206) 650-3109 (Athletic Department)

Description: Athletic scholarships for undergraduates
Restrictions: Limited to scholarships for men's and women's basketball, men's football, men's and women's soccer, men's and women's track and field and women's volleyball
$ Given: 17 awards for men and 17 awards for women ranging up to $1,500 (in-state resident tuition) and $7,000 (out-of-state resident tuition)
Deadline: Contact the department coaches
Contact: Linda Goodrich, Athletic Director

Eastern Washington University
MS 142
Cheney, WA 99004
(509) 359-2314
(509) 458-6295
(Athletic Department)

Description: Athletic scholarships for undergraduates
Restrictions: Limited to scholarships for men's and women's basketball, men's and women's cross-country running, men's football, men's and women's tennis, men's and women's track and field and women's volleyball
$ Given: 23 awards for men totalling $63,413; 10 awards for women totalling $33,120; awards ranging to full scholarships of $5,523 per year for full in-state resident scholarships (tuition, room and board) and $10,035 per year for full out-of-state resident scholarships (tuition, room and board)
Deadline: Contact the department coaches
Contact: Dick Zornes, Athletic Director

Evergreen State College
Olympia, WA 98505
(206) 866-6000 Ext. 6770
(Recreation Department)

Description: Athletic scholarships for undergraduates
Restrictions: Limited to scholarships for men's and women's soccer and men's and women's swimming
$ Given: 64 available awards for men and women ranging from partial to full tuition scholarships of $936
Deadline: Contact the department coaches
Contact: Ms. Georgette Chun, Director of Financial Aid

FREE MONEY FOR ATHLETIC SCHOLARSHIPS

Gonzaga University
East 502 Boone Avenue
Spokane, WA 99258
(509) 328-4220 Ext. 3519

Description: Athletic scholarships for undergraduates
Restrictions: Limited to scholarships for men's baseball, men's and women's basketball, men's and women's cross-country, men's and women's soccer and women's volleyball
$ Given: 21 awards for men; 26 awards for women; ranging up to full awards of $16,200 per year (in basketball)
Deadline: Contact the department coaches
Contact: Mike Roth, Assistant Athletic Director

Pacific Lutheran University
Tacoma, WA 98447
(206) 535-7161
(Financial Aid)
(206) 535-7350
(Athletic Department)

Description: Athletic scholarships for undergraduates
Restrictions: Limited to scholarships for men's and women's basketball, men's and women's cross-country running, men's football, men's golf, men's and women's cross-country skiing, men's and women's downhill skiing, women's softball, men's and women's swimming and diving, men's and women's tennis, men's and women's track and field, women's volleyball and men's wrestling
$ Given: Unspecified number of awards for men and women of varying amounts
Deadline: Contact the department coaches
Contact: Dr. Olsen, Dean of Athletic Department

Seattle Pacific University
3307 Third Avenue West
Seattle, WA 98119
(206) 281-2046 (Financial)
(206) 281-2081
(Athletic Department)

Description: Athletic scholarships for undergraduates
Restrictions: Limited to scholarships for men's and women's basketball, men's and women's cross-country running, women's gymnastics, men's soccer, men's and women's track and field and women's volleyball
$ Given: 16 awards for men and women ranging: $8,351 (partial scholarships) - $16,703 (full scholarships)
Deadline: Contact the department coaches
Contact: Mrs. Jeanne R. Rich, Director of Financial Aid

Seattle University
Seattle, WA 98122-4460
(206) 296-5840
(206) 296-6400
(Athletic Department)

Description: Athletic scholarships for undergraduates
Restrictions: Limited to scholarships for men's and women's basketball, men's and women's cross-country, men's and women's downhill skiing, men's and women's soccer and men's and women's tennis
$ Given: 15 awards for men and 20 awards for women totalling $87,112 ranging from partial awards - $12,150 per year
Deadline: Contact the department coaches
Contact: Nancy Geron, Athletic Director

University of Puget Sound
1500 North Warner Street
Tacoma, WA 98416
(206) 756-3214
(Financial Aid)
(206) 756-3140
(Athletic Department)

Description: Athletic scholarships for undergraduates
Restrictions: Limited to scholarships for men's baseball, men's and women's basketball, men's and women's cross-country running, men's football, men's golf, men's and women's soccer, women's softball, men's and women's swimming and diving, men's and women's tennis, men's and women's track and field and women's volleyball
$ Given: 33 awards for men totalling $126,000 and 27 awards for women totalling $74,000; of various amounts ranging up to full scholarships for basketball and football
Deadline: Contact the department coaches
Contact: Ms. Kathleen Vodjansky, Director of Scholarships, or Richard Ulrich, Athletic Director

University of Washington
1400 Northeast Campus
Parkway
Seattle, WA 98195
(206) 543-2210
(Athletic Department)

Description: Athletic scholarships for undergraduates
Restrictions: Limited to scholarships for men's baseball, men's and women's basketball, men's and women's crew, men's and women's cross-country running, men's football, men's and women's golf, women's gymnastics, men's and women's soccer, women's softball, men's and women's swimming and diving, men's and women's tennis, men's and women's track and field and women's volleyball
$ Given: 10 available awards for men totalling at least $146,000 and 10 available awards for women totalling at least $146,000; awards ranging from one-fourth tuition to $14,600 (for basketball, football, volleyball and women's tennis)
Deadline: Contact the department coaches
Contact: Barbara Hedges, Athletic Director

FREE MONEY FOR ATHLETIC SCHOLARSHIPS

• • • • • • • • • • • • • • • • • •

Washington State University
Administrative Suite
Streit-Perham Hall
Pullman, WA 99164-1039
(509) 335-1059
(509) 335-0271
(Scholarships)

Description: Athletic scholarships for undergraduates
Restrictions: Limited to scholarships for men's baseball, men's and women's basketball, women's crew, men's and women's cross-country running, men's football, men's and women's golf, women's soccer, women's swimming and diving, men's and women's tennis, men's and women's track and field and women's volleyball
$ Given: 72 awards for men and women ranging up to $7,000 (full in-state resident scholarship) and $12,000 (full out-of-state resident scholarship)
Deadline: Contact the department coaches
Contact: Ms. Johanna Davis, Coordinator of Scholarship Services, or Julie Health, Scholarships Office

WEST VIRGINIA

Bluefield State College
Bluefield, WV 24701
(304) 327-4501
(304) 327-4191
(Athletic Department)

Description: Athletic scholarships for undergraduates
Restrictions: Limited to scholarships for men's baseball, men's and women's basketball, men's and women's cross-country running, men's golf, women's softball and men's and women's tennis
$ Given: 40 available awards for men and women including 31 full tuition awards (5 for baseball, 20 for basketball, 3 for golf and 3 for tennis)
Deadline: Contact the department coaches
Contact: Terry Brown, Athletic Director, or Annette Osborne, Financial Aid Office

Concord College
Athens, WV 24712
(304) 384-5358
(Financial Aid)
(304) 384-5347
(Athletic Department)

Description: Athletic scholarships for undergraduates
Restrictions: Limited to scholarships for men's baseball, men's and women's basketball, men's football and women's volleyball
$ Given: 46 awards for men totalling $10,993; 21 available awards for women; ranging up to 14 full scholarships in basketball, 25 in football and 7 in volleyball ($1,906 in-state and $4,076 out-of-state tuition)
Deadline: Contact the department coaches
Contact: Ms. Patricia Harmon, Director of Financial Aid, or Don Christie, Athletic Director

Fairmont State College
Locust Avenue
Fairmont, WV 26554
(304) 367-4213
(304) 367-4220
(Athletic Department)

Description: Athletic scholarships for undergraduates
Restrictions: Limited to scholarships for men's and women's basketball, men's football, men's golf, men's and women's swimming and diving, men's and women's tennis and women's volleyball
$ Given: 37 awards for men totalling $101,146; 8 available awards for women totalling $21,869; awards ranging $746 (in-state resident tuition) - $1,906 (out-of-state resident tuition)
Deadline: Contact the department coaches
Contact: Mr. William D. Shaffer, Director of Financial Aid

Glenville State College
Glenville, WV 26351
(304) 462-7361 Ext. 152

Description: Athletic scholarships for undergraduates
Restrictions: Limited to scholarships for men's and women's basketball, men's football and men's golf
$ Given: Limited number of awards for men totalling $12,200; 3 awards for women totalling $9,150; of various amounts
Deadline: Contact the department coaches
Contact: Mr. Mack Samples, Dean of Admissions and Records

Marshall University
Old Main 122
Huntington, WV 25755
(304) 696-3162
(Financial Aid)
(304) 696-5408
(Athletic Department)

Description: Athletic scholarships for undergraduates
Restrictions: Limited to scholarships for men's and women's basketball, men's and women's cross-country running, men's football, men's golf, men's soccer, women's softball, women's tennis, men's and women's track and field and women's volleyball
$ Given: Unspecified number of available awards for men and women ranging up to $6,916 (in-state resident tuition, room and board) - $18,458 (out-of-state resident tuition, room and board)
Deadline: Contact the department coaches
Contact: Dr. Edgar W. Miller, Associate Dean of Students/ Director of Student Financial Assistance

FREE MONEY FOR ATHLETIC SCHOLARSHIPS

• • • • • • • • • • • • • • • • • • • •

Shepherd College
Shepherdstown, WV 25443
(304) 876-2511 Ext. 283

Description: Athletic scholarships for undergraduates
Restrictions: Limited to scholarships for men's and women's basketball, men's football and women's volleyball
$ Given: 15 awards for men totalling $27,370; 5 awards for women totalling $15,755 of varying amounts; maximum awards of $1,965 (semester's tuition)
Deadline: Contact the department coaches
Contact: Mr. Haydon Rudolf, Director of Financial Aid

West Liberty State College
West Liberty, WV 26074
(304) 336-8076 (Admissions)
(304) 336-8046
(Athletic Department)

Description: Athletic scholarships for undergraduates
Restrictions: Limited to scholarships for men's baseball, men's basketball, men's football, women's softball, men's and women's tennis and women's volleyball
$ Given: 11 awards for men totalling $29,070 and 2 awards for women totalling $1,080; of various amounts
Deadline: Contact the department coaches
Contact: Mr. Jim Watson, Athletic Director

West Virginia Institute of Technology
Montgomery, WV 25136
(304) 442-3228 (Financial)
(304) 442-3121 (Athletic)

Description: Athletic scholarships for undergraduates
Restrictions: Limited to scholarships for men's baseball, men's and women's basketball and men's football
$ Given: Unspecified number of available awards for men and women ranging: $100 - $1,000
Deadline: Contact the department coaches
Contact: Mrs. Nina Morton, Director of Financial Aid

West Virginia State College
Post Office Box 1000
Campus Box 187
Institute, WV 25112-1000
(304) 766-3131
(Financial Aid)
(304) 766-3165
(Athletic Department)

Description: Athletic awards and tuition waivers for undergraduates
Restrictions: Limited to scholarships for men's and women's basketball, men's football and women's softball
$ Given: Unspecified number of available awards for men and women ranging up to tuition waivers of $2,000 (in-state residents) and $4,400 (out-of-state residents)
Deadline: Contact the department coaches
Contact: Dr. Smith, Athletic Director

West Virginia University
Post Office Box 6004
Morgantown, WV 26506-6004
(304) 293-4126
(304) 293-7562 Ext. 502
(Athletic Department)

Description: Athletic scholarships for undergraduates
Restrictions: Limited to scholarships for men's baseball, men's and women's basketball, men's and women's cross-country running, men's football, women's gymnastics, men's and women's riflery, men's soccer, men's and women's swimming and diving, men's and women's tennis, men's and women's track and field, women's volleyball and men's wrestling
$ Given: 70 available awards for men totalling $219,960 and 40 available awards for women totalling $116,640; ranging $200 - $10,000 per year
Deadline: Send tape to individual coaches
Contact: Robert Shaw, Recruiting Coordinator, or Garrett Ford, Athletic Director

WISCONSIN

Marquette University
Milwaukee, WI 53233
(414) 288-7302

Description: Athletic scholarships for undergraduates
Restrictions: Limited to scholarships for men's and women's basketball, men's and women's cross-country running, men's and women's soccer, men's and women's tennis, men's and women's track and field, women's volleyball and men's wrestling
$ Given: Available awards for men and women ranging: $2,000 - 28 full awards of $15,700 each for men's and women's basketball, women's soccer and women's volleyball
Deadline: Contact the department coaches
Contact: Mr. Leo B. Flynn, Director of Admissions

University of Wisconsin - Green Bay
2420 Nicolet Drive
Green Bay, WI 54311-7001
(414) 465-2075
(Financial Aid)
(414) 465-2145
(Athletic Department)

Description: Athletic scholarships for undergraduates
Restrictions: Limited to scholarships for men's and women's basketball, men's and women's cross-country running, men's golf, men's and women's cross-country skiing, men's and women's soccer, women's swimming and diving, men's and women's tennis and women's volleyball
$ Given: 200 awards of varying amounts ranging: $6,500 - $10,000 (full awards for basketball, soccer and tennis)
Deadline: February 1. Contact the department coaches
Contact: Dan Spielmann, Athletic Director

FREE MONEY FOR ATHLETIC SCHOLARSHIPS

. . . .

**University of Wisconsin -
Madison**
432 North Murray Street
Madison, WI 53706
(608) 262-3060 (Admissions)
(608) 262-5068
(Athletic Director)

Description: Athletic scholarships for undergraduates
Restrictions: Limited to scholarships for men's and women's basketball, women's crew, men's and women's cross-country running, men's football, women's golf, men's ice hockey, men's and women's swimming and diving, men's and women's tennis, men's and women's track and field, women's volleyball and men's wrestling
$ Given: Unspecified number of available awards for men and women ranging: $200 - $12,000 per year
Deadline: Contact the department coaches
Contact: Pat Richter, Athletic Director

**University of Wisconsin -
Milwaukee**
Post Office Box 469
Milwaukee, WI 53201
(414) 229-4541
(Financial Aid)
(414) 229-5669
(Athletic Department)

Description: Athletic scholarships for undergraduates
Restrictions: Limited to scholarships for men's and women's basketball, men's and women's cross-country running, men's and women's soccer, women's softball, men's and women's swimming and diving, men's and women's tennis, men's and women's track and field and men's and women's volleyball
$ Given: Unspecified number of available awards for men and women ranging $1,200 - $11,000 per year (full awards for men's and women's basketball, men's soccer and women's volleyball)
Deadline: Contact the department coaches
Contact: Ms. Mary E. Roggeman, Director of Financial Aid, or Deanna D'Abbaccio, Compliance Officer

**University of Wisconsin -
Parkside**
900 Wood Road
Kenosha, WI 53141
(414) 595-2577
(Financial Aid)
(414) 595-2156
(Athletic Director)

Description: Athletic scholarships for undergraduates
Restrictions: Limited to scholarships for men's and women's basketball, men's and women's cross-country running, men's golf, men's soccer, men's and women's track and field, women's volleyball and men's wrestling
$ Given: 40 available awards for men totalling $80,000 and 40 available awards for women totalling $80,000; all are partial tuition scholarships of $2,000
Deadline: Contact the department coaches
Contact: Linda Draft, Athletic Director

● ●

WYOMING

University of Wyoming
Laramie, WY 82071
(307) 766-2117
(Financial Aid)

Description: Athletic scholarships for undergraduates
Restrictions: Limited to scholarships for men's baseball, men's and women's basketball, men's and women's cross-country running, men's football, men's and women's golf, men's and women's swimming and diving, men's and women's track and field, women's volleyball and men's wrestling
$ Given: 109 awards for men totalling $207,600 and 43 awards for women totalling $80,730; ranging up to $849 (semester's tuition for in-state resident) and $2,216 (semester's tuition for out-of-state resident)
Deadline: Contact the department coaches
Contact: Ms. Beth Suyematsu, Scholarship Coordinator

Athletic Associations

• •

Sports associations only infrequently provide funding for college athletes, and concentrate instead on establishing and maintaining tournament rules, keeping statistics, and distributing medals, pins, and other non-monetary awards. The following is a list of some of the main sports associations of interest to college athletes, and a brief description of their activities and programs.

FREE MONEY FOR ATHLETIC SCHOLARSHIPS

• • • • • • • • • • • • • • • • • • •

ARCHERY

National Archery Association of the United States
1750 E. Boulder St.
Colorado Springs, CO
80909-5778
(719) 578-4576

Description: Establishes and standardizes tournament rules, maintains archery records, sponsors matches. Awards medals, pins, and college scholarships of $500.
Restrictions: Must be NAA members with a minimum 2.5 GPA. Two letters of recommendation and three scores from a NAA tournament must be submitted with application.
Given: Eight $500 college scholarships.
Deadlines: October.
Contact: Christine McCartney, Executive Director.

BADMINTON

United States Badminton Association
1750 E. Boulder St., Bldg. 10
Rm. 127
Colorado Springs, CO
80909
(719) 578-4808

Description: Helps develop clubs, arranges and manages tournaments.
Restrictions: N/A
Given: Awards Thomas Cup for men and Uber Cub for women.
Deadlines: N/A
Contact: Mark Hodges, Executive Director.

BASKETBALL

U.S.A. Basketball
1750 E. Boulder St.
Colorado Springs, CO
80909-5777
(719) 632-7687

Description: The national governing body for U.S. basketball at the Pan America and Olympic competitions.
Restrictions: N/A
Given: Maintains film and photo library.
Deadlines: N/A
Contact: William L. Wall, Executive Director

BASKETBALL

Women's Basketball Coaches Association
1687 Tullie Circle, Ste. 127
Atlanta, GA 30329
(404) 321-2922

Description: Promotes and develops women's basketball.
Restrictions: N/A
Given: Sponsors eight national clinics. Bestows All America, Coach of the Year, Player of the Year.
Deadlines: N/A
Contact: Betty Jaynes, Executive Director

BOBSLED

U.S. Bobsled and Skeleton Federation
Box 828
Lake Placid, NY 12946
(518) 523-1842

Description: Promotes bobsledding and skeleton sledding in the U.S. Assembles team members for U.S. Olympic bobsled team.
Restrictions: N/A
Given: Bestows awards, conducts developmental programs.
Deadlines: N/A
Contact: Ray Pratt, Executive Director

BOWLING

Young American Bowling Alliance
5301 S. 76th St.
Greendale, WI 53129
(414) 421-4700

Description: Conducts bowling programs for those 21 years of age and under who bowl in sanctioned leagues that do not offer money or merchandise.
Restrictions: See above.
Given: Awards plaques, rings, jackets, and certificates to winners of high games, high series and other accomplishments.
Deadlines: N/A
Contact: Joseph Wilson, Executive Director

. . . .

BOXING

U.S.A. Amateur Boxing Federation
1750 E. Boulder St.
Colorado Springs, CO
80909
(719) 578-4506

Description: Promotes amateur boxing in the U.S. Conducts competitions, compiles statistics, maintains library.
Restrictions: N/A
Given: Sponsors clinics and seminars; bestows awards.
Deadlines: N/A
Contact: James J. Fox, Executive Director

EQUESTRIAN SPORTS

American Horse Shows Association
220 E. 42nd Street
Suite 409
New York, NY 10017-5876
(212) 972-2472

Description: Promotes equestrian sports in the U.S., establishes and maintains rules, administers drug programs.
Restrictions: N/A
Given: Sponsors competitions, gives referrals, provides general assistance.
Deadlines: N/A
Contact: Chrystine Jones Tauber, Executive Vice Director

Intercollegiate Horse Show Association
Smoke Run Farm
Hollow Road, Box 741
Stony Brook, NY 11790
(516) 751-2803

Description: Promotes horsemanship on the college level, stages intercollegiate competitions.
Restrictions: N/A
Given: Bestows team and individual awards, Grand Champion National Trophy.
Deadlines: N/A
Contact: Robert E. Cacchione, Executive Director

United States Equestrian Team
Gladstone, NJ 07934
(908) 234-1251

Description: Organizes riders and horses for international competitions, including the Olympic Games. Holds national competitions, including the Olympic trials.
Restrictions: N/A
Given: Trains and finances riders and horses representing the U.S. in international competitions.
Deadlines: N/A
Contact: Robert C. Standish, Executive Director

FENCING

United States Fencing Association
1750 E. Boulder St.
Colorado Springs, CO
80909
(719) 578-4511

Description: Selects fencing teams for national and international competitions, including the World University and Olympic teams, and conducts national fencing competitions.
Restrictions: N/A
Given: Sponsors such educational activities as a Junior Development Program and coaching seminars.
Deadlines: N/A
Contact: Carla-Mae Richards, Executive Director

National Intercollegiate Women's Fencing Association
3 Derby Lane
Dumont, NJ 07628
(201) 578-4511

Description: Promotes the sport of fencing among university and college women.
Restrictions: Restricted to those colleges with varsity women's fencing.
Given: Conducts clinics, workshops, and fencing competitions. Selects All-American Women's Fencing Team.
Deadlines: N/A
Contact: Sharon Everson, President

FIELD HOCKEY

Field Hockey Association of America
1750 E. Boulder St.
Colorado Springs, CO
80909
(719) 578-4587

Description: Governing body for men's field hockey in the United States.
Restrictions: N/A
Given: Sanctions tournaments and development, sponsors junior and senior national teams.
Deadlines: N/A
Contact: Edwin R. Cliatt, Executive Director

FREE MONEY FOR ATHLETIC SCHOLARSHIPS

. . . .

U.S.A. Field Hockey
Association of America
1750 E. Boulder St.
Colorado Springs, CO
80909
(719) 578-4567

Description: Governing body for women's field hockey in the United States. Promotes interest in women's field hockey in clubs, schools and colleges.
Restrictions: N/A
Given: Stages exhibition games and coaching clinics, provides technical materials and rents films. Sponsors annual national tournament.
Deadlines: N/A
Contact: Carolyn L. Moody, Executive Director

FOOTBALL

National Collegiate
Football Association
15 Tulipwood Drive
Commack, NY 11725
(516) 543-0730

Description: Promotes nonscholarship college football at the small college level.
Restrictions: N/A
Given: Selects All-American teams, promotes postseason competition.
Deadlines: N/A
Contact: Stan Gural, Commissioner

GOLF

All-American Collegiate
Golf Foundation
555 Madison Avenue, 12th Fl.
New York, NY 10022
(212) 751-5170

Description: Promotes golf at the college level.
Restrictions: N/A
Given: Presents awards. Scholarships are given to students (not necessarily golfing students) with money raised from golfing events.
Deadlines: N/A
Contact: Karen Boyer

Golf Coaches Association
of America
Ohio State University
3605 Tremont Rd.
Columbus, OH 43221
(614) 459-4653

Description: Promotes intercollegiate and intramural golf, and arranges collegiate golf tournaments.
Restrictions: Membership restricted to golf coaches of four-year universities who are members of the NCAA.
Given: Selects All-American teams.
Deadlines: N/A
Contact: Jim Brown, President

• •

United States Golf Association
P.O. Box 708
Far Hills, NJ 07931
(908) 234-2300

Description: Governing body for golf in the United States.
Restrictions: N/A
Given: Sponsors teams for international competitions, maintains library and museum, provides advice and data on rules, amateur status, and golfing implements.
Deadlines: N/A
Contact: David B. Fay, Executive Director

GYMNASTICS

National Association of Collegiate Gymnastics Coaches (Men)
Southern Connecticut State University
Department of Physical Education
501 Crescent St.
New Haven, CT 06515
(203) 397-4245

Description: Incudes gymnastics coaches at every level. Promotes the sport, maintains hall of fame and museum, compiles statistics on college competitions.
Restrictions: N/A
Given: Presents All-America awards to college athletes, sponsors competitions.
Deadlines: N/A
Contact: A.B. Crossfield

United States Gymnastics Federation
201 S. Capitol
Suite 300
Indianapolis, IN 46225
(317) 237-5050

Description: Selects teams for international competitions, including the Olympic Games.
Restrictions: N/A
Given: Conducts training sessions, bestows awards, compiles statistics.
Deadlines: N/A
Contact: Mike Jacki, Executive Director

HANDBALL

United States Handball Association
930 N. Benton Avenue
Tucson, AZ 85711
(602) 795-0434

Description: Includes players and coaches; promotes intercollegiate handball.
Restrictions: N/A
Given: Sponsors tournaments.
Deadlines: N/A
Contact: Robert C. Peters, Commissioner

• • • • • • • • • • • • • • • • • • •

HOCKEY

Central Collegiate Hockey Association
100 S. State Street
Ann Arbor, MI 48109
(313) 764-2590

Description: Includes the Division I hockey programs at Bowling Green State University, Ferris State University, Kent Sate University, Lake Superior State University, Michigan State University, Miami University of Ohio, Ohio State University, University of Illinois at Chicago, University of Michigan, and Western Michigan University.
Restrictions: See above.
Given: Sponsors competitions, bestows awards.
Deadlines: N/A
Contact: Bill Beagan, Commissioner

Eastern College Hockey Association
1311 Craigville Beach Road
P.O. Box 3
Centerville, MA 02632
(508) 771-5060

Description: Organization for Eastern colleges with ice hockey teams.
Restrictions: See above.
Given: Maintains records, supervises scheduling.
Deadlines: N/A
Contact: Clayton W. Chapman, Commissioner

U.S.A. Hockey
2997 Broadmoor Valley Rd.
Colorado Springs, CO 80906
(719) 576-4990

Description: The governing body for U.S. amateur hockey.
Restrictions: N/A
Given: Organizes tournaments, sponsors clinics, maintains statistics, awards trophies.
Deadlines: N/A
Contact: Baaron B. Pittenger, Executive Director

Western Collegiate Hockey Association
P.O. Box 14599
Madison, WI 53714
(608) 251-4003

Description: Includes the hockey programs at Colorado College, Michigan Technological University, Northern Michigan University, St. Cloud State University, University of Denver, University of Minnesota, University of Minnesota-Duluth, University of North Dakota, and University of Wisconsin.
Restrictions: See above.
Given: Supervises games, compiles statistics, bestows awards.
Deadlines: N/A
Contact: Otto Breitenbach, Commissioner

JAI ALAI

United States Amateur Jai Alai Players Association
1935 N.E. 150th Street
North Miami, FL 33181
(305) 944-8217

Description: Promotes the sport of jai alai in the U.S.
Restrictions: N/A
Given: Sends U.S. teams to international competitions.
Deadlines: N/A
Contact: Howard Kalik, Director

JUDO

United States Judo
P.O. Box 10013
El Paso, TX 79991
(915) 565-8754

Description: Governing body for amateur judo in the U.s.
Restrictions: N/A
Given: Sponsors competitions, bestows awards.
Deadlines: N/A
Contact: Frank P. Fullerton, President

United States Judo Association
19 North Union Boulevard
Colorado Springs, CO 80909
(719) 633-7750

Description: Promotes amateur judo in the U.S., sponsors tournaments.
Restrictions: N/A
Given: Through the National Judo Institute, offers training and tournaments. Recognizes outstanding male and female judo athletes of the year.
Deadlines: N/A
Contact: Larry Lee, Executive Director

KARATE

U.S.A. Karate Federation
1300 Kenmore Boulevard
Akron, OH 44314
(216) 753-3114

Description: U.S. governing body for karate. Selects national U.S. karate team.
Restrictions: N/A
Given: Organizes competitions, conducts classes, bestows awards.
Deadlines: N/A
Contact: George E. Anderson, President

FREE MONEY FOR ATHLETIC SCHOLARSHIPS

LACROSSE

Lacrosse Foundation
113 West University
Parkway
Baltimore, MD 21210
(301) 235-6882

Description: Promotes men's and women's lacrosse.
Restrictions: N/A
Given: Maintains educational programs, bestows awards.
Deadlines: N/A
Contact: Steve Stenersen, Executive Director

United States Intercollegiate Lacrosse Association
Washington and Lee
University
P.O. Box 928
Lexington, VA 24450
(703) 463-8670

Description: Promotes lacrosse on the college level.
Restrictions: See above.
Given: Bestows awards, sponsors competitions.
Deadlines: N/A
Contact: Chuck O'Connell, Secretary

United States Women's Lacrosse Association
45 Maple Avenue
Hamilton, NY 13346
(315) 824-2480

Description: Promotes women's lacrosse.
Restrictions: N/A
Given: Sponsors national and international events, bestows awards, conducts clinics.
Deadlines: N/A
Contact: Susanna McVaugh, Executive Secretary

LUGE

United States Luge Association
P.O. Box 651
Lake Placid, NY 12946
(518) 523-2071

Description: Promotes luge in the U.S., selects luge athletes for U.S. Olympic team.
Given: Bestows awards, conducts seminars, helps defray training expenses of amateur athletes.
Deadlines: N/A
Contact: Ronald Rossi, Executive Director

• •

OLYMPICS

United States Olympic Committee
1750 E. Boulder Street
Colorado Springs, CO
80909
(719) 632-5551

Description: National governing body of the thirty-seven sports represented in the Olympic Games. Holds U.S. Olympic Festival every year but Olympic year, maintains two Olympic training centers.
Restrictions: See above.
Given: College Olympic athletes are eligible for up to $5,000 in tuition assistance grants. At the U.S. Olympic Education Center Olympic athletes competing in badminton, biathlon, boxing, skiing and speedskating can pursue academic and athletic goals simultaneously at Northern Michigan University in Marquette, Michigan. At the two U.S. Olympic training centers in Colorado Springs and Lake Placid Olympic students are eligible for in-state tuition and other support. The Athlete Education Mentoring Network is also maintained to counsel athletes on academic and financial issues. In addition, the Olympic athlete may be eligible for tuition reimbursement and job placement services. The USOC also maintains a number of programs for Olympians at the end of their athletic careers.
Deadlines: N/A
Contact: 1-800-933-4473

POLO

United States Polo Association
Kentucky Horse Park
4059 Iron Works Pike
Lexington, KY 40511
(606) 255-0593

Description: A federation of polo clubs.
Restrictions: N/A
Given: Maintains polo schools.
Deadlines: N/A
Contact: Allan D. Scherer, Executive Director

. . . .

POWERLIFTING

U.S. Powerlifting Federation
P.O. Box 389
Roy, UT 84067
(801) 825-5826

Description: Promotes powerlifting through sanctioned competitions.
Restrictions: N/A
Given: Sponsors seminars and clinics, bestows awards.
Deadlines: N/A
Contact: Jan Shendow, President

RACQUETBALL

American Amateur Racquetball Association
815 North Weber
Suite 101
Colorado Springs, CO
80903
(719) 635-5396

Description: Promotes racquetball by sponsoring events both nationally and internationally.
Restrictions: N/A
Given: Sponsors competitions, bestows awards.
Deadlines: N/A
Contact: Luke St. Onge, Executive Director

RODEO

National Intercollegiate Rodeo Association
1815 Portland Avenue, No. 3
Walla Walla, WA 99362
(509) 529-4402

Description: An organization of college rodeo clubs and college rodeo participants.
Restrictions: See above.
Given: Sponsors the annual College National Finals Rodeo.
Deadlines: N/A
Contact: Timothy Corfield, Executive Secretary

ROWING

Eastern Association of Rowing Colleges
1311 Craigville Beach Road
P.O. Box 3
Centerville, MA 02632
(508) 771-5060

Description: Colleges with rowing teams.
Restrictions: See above.
Given: Sponsors May regatta for eight-oared shells, awards trophy.
Deadlines: N/A
Contact: Clayton W. Chapman, Secretary-Treasurer

. . . .

Intercollegiate Rowing Association
1311 Craigville Beach Road
P.O. Box 3
Centerville, MA 02632
(508) 771-5060

Description: Colleges promoting intercollegiate rowing championship.
Restrictions: See above.
Given: Sponsors June regatta in Syracuse, New York.
Deadlines: N/A
Contact: Clayton W. Chapman, Secretary-Treasurer

National Rowing Foundation
P.O. Box 10
Newington, VA 22122-0010
(703) 379-2974

Description: Promotes the sport of rowing in the U.S.
Restrictions: N/A
Given: Sponsors an international regatta and a national team.
Deadlines: N/A
Contact: Jack T. Franklin, Executive Secretary-Treasurer

United States Rowing Association
201 S. Capitol Avenue
Suite 400
Indianapolis, IN 46225
(317) 237-5656

Description: U.S. governing body for Olympic rowing. Selects men's and women's crews to participate in international competitions, including the Olympics.
Restrictions: N/A
Given: Runs clinics, bestows awards.
Deadlines: N/A
Contact: Paula Oyer, Executive Director

RUGBY

United States of America Rugby Football Union
3595 E. Fountain Boulevard
Colorado Springs, CO 80910
(719) 637-1022

Description: A national organization comprising four regional rugby unions.
Restrictions: N/A
Given: Conducts clinics, fields national team.
Deadlines: N/A
Contact: Karen Kast, Director of Administration

FREE MONEY FOR ATHLETIC SCHOLARSHIPS

. . . .

SHOOTING

National Rifle Association of America
1600 Rhode Island Avenue N.W.
Washington, D.C. 20036
(202) 828-6000

Description: Promotes shooting and marksmanship.
Restrictions: N/A
Given: Sponsors U.S. teams in international competition, bestows awards.
Deadlines: N/A
Contact: Wayne R. LaPierre, Jr., Executive Vice President

SKATING

Amateur Skating Union of the United States
1033 Shady Lane
Glen Ellyn, IL 60137
(708) 790-3230

Description: Promotes ice speed skating in the United States.
Restrictions: See above.
Given: Conducts seminars, compiles statistics.
Deadlines: N/A
Contact: Shirley A. Yates, Executive Secretary

United States Figure Skating Association
20 First Street
Colorado Springs, CO 80906
(719) 635-5200

Description: Governing body for amateur U.S. figure skating.
Restrictions: See above.
Given: Compiles statistics, bestows awards.
Deadlines: N/A
Contact: Ian Anderson, Executive Director

United States International Speed Skating Association
240 Oneida Street
Syracuse, NY 13204

Description: Promotes Olympic style speed skating, and selects U.S. Olympic team.
Restrictions: N/A
Given: Sponsors competitions, bestows awards.
Deadlines: N/A
Contact: John Byrne, Executive Officer

SKIING

National Collegiate Ski Association
P.O. Box 100
Park City, UT 84060
(801) 649-9090

Description: Promotes both competitive and recreational skiing at the college level.
Restrictions: See above.
Given: Sponsors competitions, bestows awards.
Deadlines: N/A
Contact: Howard Petersen, President

United States Ski Team Foundation
P.O. Box 100
Park City, UT 84060
(801) 649-9090

Description: Promotes interest in the U.S. in both national and international competitions.
Restrictions: N/A
Given: College tuition assistance to current and former athletes.
Deadlines: N/A
Contact: Jennifer Stevens, Director of Development

United States Skiing
P.O. Box 100
Park City, UT 84060
(801) 649-9090

Description: Governing body for Olympic skiing in the U.S.
Restrictions: N/A
Given: Administers competitions.
Deadlines: N/A
Contact: Howard Peterson

SOCCER

Intercollegiate Soccer Association of America
1821 Sunny Drive
St. Louis, MO 63122
(314) 349-1967

Description: Promotes soccer on the college level.
Restrictions: N/A
Given: Bestows awards, rates soccer teams weekly.
Deadlines: N/A
Contact: Bill Coulthart, Executive Secretary

• •

SOFTBALL

Amateur Softball Association of America
2801 N.E. 50th St.
Oklahoma City, OK 73111-7203
(405) 424-5266

Description: Governing body for softball in the U.S.
Restrictions: N/A
Given: Conducts competitions and clinics; bestows awards.
Deadlines: N/A
Contact: Don E. Porter, Executive Director

SQUASH

National Intercollegiate Squash Racquets Association
Vassar College Athletic Department
P.O. Box 402
Poughkeepsie, NY 12601
(914) 437-7467

Description: An organization of colleges in the U.S. and Canada with squash teams.
Restrictions: See above.
Given: Bestows awards, stages competition.
Deadlines: N/A
Contact: Bill Barhite, Vice President

SURFING

Eastern Surfing Association
P.O. Box 582
Ocean City, MD 21842
(301) 289-0515

Description: Promotes the sport of amateur surfing through competitions.
Restrictions: See above.
Given: Bestows awards.
Deadlines: N/A
Contact: Kathlyn B. Phillips, Executive Director

Hawaii Surfing Association
3107 Lincoln Avenue
Honolulu, HI 96816
(808) 737-0231

Description: Promotes surfing on the high school and college levels.
Restrictions: Restricted to those who have competed in at least one sanctioned meet.
Given: Prepares amateurs for professional meets, conducts seminars.
Deadlines: N/A
Contact: Anthony Guerrero, President

• • • • • • • • • • • • • • • • •

**National Scholastic
Surfing Association**
P.O. Box 495
Huntington Beach, CA
92648
(213) 592-2285

Description: Promotes high school and college competitions and international exchange trips.
Restrictions: See above.
Given: Awards scholarships to student surfers.
Deadlines: N/A
Contact: Janice Aragon, Executive Director

**United States Surfing
Federation**
7104 Island Village Drive
Long Beach, CA 90803
(213) 596-7785

Description: Governing body for U.S. amateur surfing.
Restrictions: See above.
Given: Stages national championships, picks teams for international competitions.
Deadlines: N/A
Contact: Bob Pace, President

**Women's International
Surfing Association**
30202 Silver Spur Road
P.O. Box 512
San Juan Capistrano, CA
92693
(714) 493-2591

Description: Promotes women's amateur and professional surfing in the U.S.
Restrictions: See above.
Given: Sponsors competitions and instructional programs.
Deadlines: N/A
Contact: Mary Lou Drummy, President

SWIMMING

U.S. Aquatic Sports
1750 E. Boulder Street
Colorado Springs, CO
80909
(719) 578-4578

Description: Umbrella organization for U.S. Diving, U.S. Synchronized Swimming, U.S. Swimming, and U.S. Water Polo.
Restrictions: See above.
Given: Bestows awards.
Deadlines: N/A
Contact: Ralph W. Hale, President

• • • • • • • • • • • • • • • • • • •

United States
Synchronized Swimming
Pan American Plaza
201 South Capitol
Suite 510
Indianapolis, IN 46225
(317) 237-5700

Description: Promotes synchronized swimming in the U.S.
Restrictions: N/A
Given: Bestows awards, promotes competitions.
Deadlines: N/A
Contact: Betty Watanabe, Executive Director

TABLE TENNIS

United States Table
Tennis Association
1750 E. Boulder Street
Colorado Springs, CO
80909
(719) 578-4583

Description: Assembles U.S. teams for international competitions.
Restrictions: N/A
Given: Sanctions tournaments.
Deadlines: N/A
Contact: Daniel Seemiller, President

TAEKWONDO

U.S. Taekwondo Union
1750 E. Boulder Street
Suite 405
Colorado Springs, CO
80909
(719) 578-4632

Description: Promotes taekwondo in the U.S. and represents the U.S. in international competitions.
Restrictions: N/A
Given: Sponsors competitions, conducts seminars, bestows awards.
Deadlines: N/A
Contact: Robert K. Fujimura, Executive Director

• • • • • • • • • • • • • • • • • • • •

TENNIS

Intercollegiate Tennis Coaches Association
P.O. Box 71
Princeton, NJ 08544
(609) 258-6332

Description: An organization of college tennis coaches that promotes intercollegiate tennis.
Restrictions: See above.
Given: Sponsors tournaments, bestows awards.
Deadlines: N/A
Contact: David A. Benjamin, Executive Director

United States Tennis Association
1212 Avenue of the Americas
New York, NY 10036
(212) 302-3322

Description: Promotes amateur and professional tennis in the U.S.
Restrictions: N/A
Given: Sponsors amateur and professional tennis tournaments in the U.S. for all age groups. Compiles statistics.
Deadlines: N/A
Contact: M. Marshall Happer, III, Executive Director

TRACK AND FIELD

Athletics Congress of the U.S.A.
200 Jenkins Court
Jenkintown, PA 19046-2627
(215) 887-0200

Description: Governing body for track and field, distance running, and race walking in the U.S.
Restrictions: N/A
Given: Sponsors international competitions, bestows awards.
Deadlines: N/A
Contact: Frank Greensberg, President

Triathlon Federation/U.S.A.
3595 East Fountain Boulevard
Colorado Springs, CO 80910
(719) 597-9090

Description: Promotes triathlon competition in the U.S.
Restrictions: N/A
Given: Supervises triathlons in the U.S. and internationally, chooses U.S. Ironman designates.
Deadlines: N/A
Contact: Mark Sisson, Executive Director

• • • • • • • • • • • • • • • • • • •

U.S. Biathlon Association
P.O. Box 5515
Essex Junction, VT 05453
(802) 655-4524

Description: The governing body for biathlon in the U.S. Selects biathletes for international competition, including the Olympics.
Restrictions: N/A
Given: Stages competitions, maintains training camps.
Deadlines: N/A
Contact: Howard R. Buxton, President

United States Modern Pentathlon Association
P.O. Drawer 8178
San Antonio, TX 78208
(512) 246-3000

Description: The U.S. governing body for the pentathlon, a combined competition that includes the sports of horseback riding, fencing, pistol shooting, swimming, and cross-country running. Chooses competitors for international events, including the Olympics.
Restrictions: N/A
Given: Bestows awards, designates All-American team.
Deadlines: N/A
Contact: William Hanson, Executive Director

TRAINERS

American Athletic Trainers Association and Certification Board
660 West Duarte Road
Arcadia, CA 91007
(818) 445-1978

Description: Establishes standards and certifies athletic trainers.
Restrictions: N/A
Given: Conducts educational programs, maintains a placement service, and bestows Trainer of the Year award.
Deadlines: N/A
Contact: Joe S. Borland, Board Chairman

National Athletic Trainers Association
2952 Stemmons Freeway
Suite 200
Dallas, TX 75274-6103
(214) 637-6282

Description: An organization that includes trainers at all levels of amateur and professional sports.
Restrictions: N/A
Given: Bestows awards and scholarships.
Deadlines: N/A
Contact: Alan A. Smith, Jr., Executive Director

National Strength and Conditioning Association
P.O. Box 81410
Lincoln, NE 68501
(402) 472-3000

Description: Promotes strength and conditioning training as both a contributor to the athlete's performance and to his or her overall health.
Restrictions: N/A
Given: Conducts workshops, certification programs.
Deadlines: N/A
Contact: Ken Kontor, Executive Director

UNDERWATER SPORTS

Underwater Society of America
P.O. Box 628
Daly City, CA 94017
(415) 583-8492

Description: Promotes all underwater sports in the U.S., as well as scientific aspects of underwater diving.
Restrictions: N/A
Given: Bestows awards, stages competitions.
Deadlines: N/A
Contact: George Rose, President

VOLLEYBALL

United States Volleyball Association
3595 E. Fountain Boulevard
Colorado Springs, CO
80910-1740
(719) 637-8300

Description: Governing body for volleyball in the U.S.
Restrictions: N/A
Given: Sponsors men's and women's Olympic teams.
Deadlines: N/A
Contact: William W. Baird, President

WATER POLO

United States Water Polo
201 South Capitol
Suite 520
Indianapolis, IN 46225
(317) 237-5599

Description: Promotes water polo in the U.S.
Restrictions: N/A
Given: Conducts clinics, bestows awards, sponsors competitions.
Deadlines: N/A
Contact: Rich Foster, President

• •

WRESTLING

National Wrestling Coaches Association
c/o Exercise of Sport Science
University of Utah
HPR No. 250
Salt Lake City, UT 84112
(801) 581-3836

Description: An association of coaches and officials of amateur wrestling that promotes intercollegiate wrestling.
Restrictions: N/A
Given: Bestows awards.
Deadlines: N/A
Contact: Marvin G. Hess, Executive Vice President

U.S.A. Wrestling
225 S. Academy Boulevard
Colorado Springs, CO 80910
(719) 597-8333

Description: Governing body for U.S. Olympic wrestling.
Restrictions: N/A
Given: Conducts clinics, maintains film library and speakers' bureau.
Deadlines: N/A
Contact: David C. Miller, Executive Director

SPORTS ASSOCIATIONS AND CONFERENCES

Amateur Athletic Union of the United States
3400 W. 86th St.
P.O. Box 68207
Indianapolis, IN 46268
(317) 872-2900

Description: Represents fifty-eight regional groups.
Restrictions: See above.
Given: Bestows awards.
Deadlines: N/A
Contact: Stan Hooley

Athletic and Educational Opportunities/International Center
P.O. Box 31113
Chicago, IL 60631-0113

Description: Provides counseling assistance to high school and college athletes.
Restrictions: N/A
Given: Conducts seminars for students, coaches, and parents on athletics and academics.
Deadlines: N/A
Contact: Michael B. Denzel, President

Atlantic Coast Conference
P.O. Drawer ACC
Greensboro, NC 27419-6199
(919) 854-8787

Description: A nine member conference that includes Clemson University, Duke University, Florida State University, Georgia Institute of Technology, North Carolina State University, University of Maryland, University of North Carolina, University of Virginia, Wake Forest University.
Restrictions: See above.
Given: Promotes men's and women's athletics in ACC.
Deadlines: N/A
Contact: Eugene F. Corrigan, Commissioner

Big East Conference
56 Exchange Terrace
Providence, RI 02903
(401) 272-9108

Description: A twelve member conference that includes Boston College, Georgetown University, Providence College, St. John's University, Seton Hall University, Syracuse University, University of Connecticut, University of Pittsburgh, Villanova University.
Restrictions: See above.
Given: Promotes men's and women's athletics in Big East Conference.
Deadlines: N/A
Contact: Michael A. Tranghese, Commissioner

Big Eight Conference
104 W. 9th. Street
Suite 408
Kansas City, MO 64105
(816) 471-5088

Description: An eight member conference that includes Iowa State University, Kansas State University, Oklahoma State University, University of Colorado, University of Kansas, University of Missouri, University of Nebraska, University of Oklahoma.
Restrictions: See above.
Given: Promotes men's and women's athletics in Big Eight Conference.
Deadlines: N/A
Contact: Carl James, Commissioner

FREE MONEY FOR ATHLETIC SCHOLARSHIPS

• • • • • • • • • • • • • • • • • • • •

Big Ten Conference
1500 W. Higgins Road
Park Ridge, IL 60068
(708) 696-1010

Description: A midwestern conference that includes ten state universities and a private university.
Restrictions: See above.
Given: Promotes Big Ten competitions.
Deadlines: N/A
Contact: James A. Haney, Commissioner

Central Intercollegiate Athletic Association
P.O. Box 7349
Hampton, VA 23666
(804) 865-0071

Description: Promotes athletics among fourteen colleges and universities.
Restrictions: N/A
Given: See above.
Deadlines: N/A
Contact: Leon Kerry, Commissioner

Council of Ivy Group Presidents
120 Alexander Street
Princeton, NJ 08544
(609) 258-6426

Description: A six member conference that includes Brown University, Columbia University, Cornell University, Darmouth College, Harvard University, Princeton University, University of Pennsylvania, and Yale University.
Restrictions: See above.
Given: Sponsors competitions in a variety of sports.
Deadlines: N/A
Contact: Jeffrey H. Orleans, Executive Director

Metropolitan Collegiate Athletic Conference
2 Ravinia Drive
Suite 210
Atlanta, GA 30346
(404) 395-6444

Description: A sports conference that includes Tulane University, University of Louisville, University of North Carolina, Charlotte, University of South Florida, University of Southern Mississippi, Virginia Commonwealth University, and Virginia Polytechnic Institute.
Restrictions: See above.
Given: Sponsors competitions in men's and women's sports.
Deadlines: N/A
Contact: Ralph McFillen, Commissioner

. . . .

National Association of Intercollegiate Athletics
1221 Baltimore
Suite 1100
Kansas City, MO 64105
(816) 842-5050

Description: Promotes intercollegiate athletic programs, coordinates rules and standards at the national level.
Restrictions: N/A
Given: Sponsors national championships for both men and women, conducts workshops.
Deadlines: N/A
Contact: James R. Chasteen, President

National Christian College Athletic Association
P.O. Box 1312
Marion, IN 46952
(317) 674-8401

Description: Promotes athletic competition among seven evangelical Christian colleges.
Restrictions: See above.
Given: Bestows awards, compiles statistics.
Deadlines: N/A
Contact: Barry R. May, Executive Director

National Collegiate Athletic Association
6201 College Boulevard
Overland Park, KS 66211
(913) 339-1906

Description: The major governing body of amateur athletic competition in the U.S., NCAA membership consists of over a thousand colleges, universities, and educational athletic associations.
Restrictions: N/A
Given: Maintains over sixty athletic committees in men's and women's sports.
Deadlines: N/A
Contact: Richard D. Schultz, Executive Director

National Junior College Athletic Association
P.O. Box 7305
Colorado Springs, CO 80933-7305
(719) 590-9788

Description: Promotes junior college athletics on the regional and the national levels.
Restrictions: See above.
Given: Sponsors national tournaments, bestows awards.
Deadlines: N/A
Contact: George E. Killian, Executive Director

FREE MONEY FOR ATHLETIC SCHOLARSHIPS

• • • • • • • • • • • • • • • • • • • •

National Small College Athletic Association
1884 College Heights
New Ulm, MN 56073
(507) 359-9791

Description: Promotes athletics in colleges with few than 1,000 full-time students.
Restrictions: See above.
Given: Bestows awards, selects All-American basketball team.
Deadlines: N/A
Contact: Gary Dallmann

Pacific 10 Conference
800 S. Broadway
Suite 400
Walnut Creek, CA 94596
(415) 932-4411

Description: A ten member conference that includes Arizona State University, Oregon State University, Stanford University, University of Arizona, University of California, Berkeley, University of California, Los Angeles, University of Oregon, University of Southern California, University of Washington, and Washington State University.
Restrictions: See above.
Given: Sponsors competitions in men's and women's sports.
Deadlines: N/A
Contact: Thomas C. Hansen, Commissioner

Southeastern Conference
2201 Civic Center Boulevard
Birmingham, AL 35203
(205) 458-3000

Description: A twelve member conference that includes Auburn University, Louisiana State University, Mississippi State University, University of Alabama, University of Arkansas, University of Florida, University of Georgia, University of Kentucky, University of Mississippi, University of South Carolina, University of Tennessee, and Vanderbilt University.
Restrictions: See above.
Given: Sponsors competitions in men's and women's sports.
Deadlines: N/A
Contact: Roy F. Kramer, Commissioner

. . . .

Southern Conference
10 Woodfin Street
Suite 206
Asheville, NC 28801
(704) 255-7872

Description: A ten member athletic conference.
Restrictions: N/A
Given: Sponsors intercollegiate competitions.
Deadlines: N/A
Contact: Wright Waters, Commissioner

Southwest Athletic Conference
P.O. Box 569420
Dallas, TX 75356
(214) 634-7353

Description: A nine member athletic conference that includes Baylor University, Rice University, Southern Methodist University, Texas A&M University, Texas Christian University, Texas Tech University, University of Houston, and University of Texas at Austin.
Restrictions: See above.
Given: Sponsors competitions in men's and women's sports.
Deadlines: N/A
Contact: Fred Jacoby, Commissioner

United States Athletes Association
3735 Lakeland Avenue North
Suite 230
Minneapolis, MN 55422
(612) 522-5844

Description: Accents community service and promotes drug-free lifestyles among athletes in high school and in college. Encourages competition among chapters.
Restrictions: N/A
Given: Bestows awards, offers job placement assistance.
Deadlines: N/A
Contact: Carl Eller, Executive Director

United States Collegiate Sports Council
Brandeis University
Waltham, MA 02254
(617) 736-3657

Description: Encourages the participation of U.S. collegiate athletes in international competitions.
Restrictions: See above.
Given: Sponsors international competitions.
Deadlines: N/A
Contact: Nicholas Rodis, Executive Director

FREE MONEY FOR ATHLETIC SCHOLARSHIPS

• •

University Athletic Association
668 Mt. Hope Avenue
Rochester, NY 14620
(716) 275-3814

Description: A nine member athletic conference that includes Brandeis University, Carnegie Mellon University, Case Western Reserve University, Emory University, Johns Hopkins University, New York University, University of Chicago, University of Rochester, and Washington University.
Restrictions: See above.
Given: Bestows awards.
Deadlines: N/A
Contact: Richard A. Rasmussen, Executive Secretary

Western Athletic Conference
14 West Dry Creek Circle
Littleton, CO 80120-4478
(303) 795-1962

Description: A nine member athletic conference that includes United States Air Force Academy, Brigham Young University, Colorado State University, University of Hawaii, University of New Mexico, San Diego State University, University of Texas-El Paso, University of Utah, and University of Wyoming.
Restrictions: See above.
Given: Sponsors competitions in men's and women's sports.
Deadlines: N/A
Contact: Joseph L. Kearney, Commissioner

Women's Sports Foundation
342 Madison Avenue
Suite 728
New York, NY 10173
(212) 972-9170

Description: Promotes the participation of women in sports, and enforcement of Title IX of the Equal Education Act.
Restrictions: See above.
Given: Bestows awards, provides information on women's sports.
Deadlines: N/A
Contact: Deborah Anderson, Executive Director

Bibliography

. . . .

General and Undergraduate

ARCO's College Financial Aid Annual, edited by John Schwartz. New York: ARCO Publishing, Inc., 1990.
Chronicle Student Aid Annual: For 1990-91 Schoolyear. Moravia, NY: Chronicle Guidance Publications.
College Blue Book. New York: MacMillan, 1991, 23rd edition.
Financing a College Education: The Essential Guide for the 90's, by Judith B. Margolin. New York: Plenum Press, 1989.
Free Money for Athletic Scholarships, by Laurie Blum. New York: Henry Holt and Co, Inc., 1993
Free Money for College, by Laurie Blum. New York: Facts on File, 1992.
Free Money for College from the Federal Government, by Laurie Blum. New York: Henry Holt and Co, Inc., 1993
Free Money for Foreign Study, by Laurie Blum. New York: Facts on File, 1991.
Free Money for Private Schools, by Laurie Blum. New York: Simon & Schuster, 1992
Free Money from Colleges and Universities, by Laurie Blum. New York: Henry Holt and Co, Inc., 1993
National Guide to Funding for Elementary and Secondary Education. New York: The Foundation Center, 1991.
1992 Guide to Funding for Education, edited by James Marshall. Virginia: Educational Funding Research Council, 1992.
Peterson's Guide to Four-Year Colleges 1991. Princeton, NJ: Peterson's Guides, 1990.
Scholarships, Fellowships and Loans 1992-93, by Debra McKinley. Detroit: Gale Research, 1991.

Graduate, Postgraduate, and Research

Free Money for Graduate School, (revised edition) by Laurie Blum. New York: Henry Holt and Co, Inc., 1993
The Directory of Research Grants. Phoenix: Oryx Press, annual.
The Graduate Scholarship Book: The Complete Guide to Scholarships, Fellowships, Grants and Loans for Graduate and Professional Study. Englewood Cliffs, NJ: Prentice-Hall, 1990.
The Grants Register. New York: St. Martin's Press, published twice/year.

U.S. Government Support

Free Dollars from the Federal Government, by Laurie Blum. New York: ARCO Publishing, Inc., 1991.

Index

INDEX

INDEX

INDEX